LADEES AND GENTLEMEN!
BUFFALO BILL'S WILD WEST SHOW.
Plus the down-to-earth events
that made the American frontier!

My name is William F. Cody, Buffalo Bill to you. I got a legend to live up to. It was created by a dime novelist, Ned Buntline, who presented me as a lying, drinking, whoring man. A pack of lies. But never mind. Come in and see my show. It's a great, original and heroic enterprise of inimitable luster! It's got the top acts. Annie Oakley, the world's most famous woman marksman. Munoz and Manuel, the Mexican whip and fast-draw act. Daredevil cowboy trick riders. And of course Buck Taylor, King of the Cowboys. Plus hundreds of brave cowboys and fierce Indians, including Chief Sitting Bull.

WELCOME TO SHOW BUSINESS,
IT AIN'T THAT MUCH DIFFERENT
THAN REAL LIFE.

Dino De Laurentiis Presents

BUFFALO BILL AND THE INDIANS
OR
SITTING BULL'S HISTORY LESSON

PLAYERS

The Star	PAUL NEWMAN
The Producer	JOEL GREY
The Publicist	KEVIN McCARTHY
The Relative	HARVEY KEITEL
The Journalist	ALLAN NICHOLLS
The Sure Shot	GERALDINE CHAPLIN
The Sure Shot's Manager	JOHN CONSIDINE
The Wrangler	ROBERT DOQUI
The Treasurer	MIKE KAPLAN
The Bartender	BERT REMSEN
The Mezzo-Contralto	BONNIE LEADERS
The Lyric-Coloratura	NOELLE ROGERS
The Indian Agent	DENVER PYLE
The Indian	FRANK KAQUITTS
The Interpreter	WILL SAMPSON
The Arenic Director	KEN KROSSA
The King of the Cowboys	FRED N. LARSEN
The Cowboy Trick Riders	JERRI & JOY DUCE
The Mexican Whip and Fast Draw Act . . . ALEX GREEN & GARY MacKENZIE	
The Old Soldier	HUMPHREY GRATZ
The President of the United States . .	PAT McCORMICK
The First Lady	SHELLEY DUVALL
And	
The Legend Maker	BURT LANCASTER

Producer & Director
ROBERT ALTMAN

Screen Story and Screenplay by
ALAN RUDOLPH & ROBERT ALTMAN

Executive Producer
DAVID SUSSKIND

UNITED ARTISTS
Entertainment from Transamerica Corporation

BUFFALO BILL AND THE INDIANS
OR
SITTING BULL'S HISTORY LESSON

suggested by the play
"INDIANS"
Written By
ARTHUR KOPIT

Screen Story and Screenplay By
ALAN RUDOLPH
&
ROBERT ALTMAN

BANTAM BOOKS · TORONTO · LONDON · NEW YORK

BUFFALO BILL AND THE INDIANS
OR SITTING BULL'S HISTORY LESSON
A Bantam Book / July 1976

Photos by Jean Pagliuso

Cover art by Dan Perri

ISBN 0-553-10047-5

Published simultaneously in the United States and Canada

Bantam Books are published by Bantam Books, Inc. Its trade-
mark, consisting of the words "Bantam Books" and the por-
trayal of a bantam, is registered in the United States Patent
Office and in other countries. Marca Registrada. Bantam
Books, Inc., 666 Fifth Avenue, New York, New York 10019.

PRINTED IN THE UNITED STATES OF AMERICA

BUFFALO BILL AND THE INDIANS
OR
SITTING BULL'S HISTORY LESSON

BUFFALO BILL AND THE INDIANS
OR SITTING BULL'S HISTORY LESSON

A Synopsis By
THE HON. WILLIAM F. CODY
(PAUL NEWMAN)

As Told To
Alan Rudolph & Robert Altman

I, William F. Cody, Buffalo Bill (Paul Newman) to most of you, was the undisputed Lion of the Show Business in 1885. As a matter of fact I was the Lion of the Show Business before the show business was invented. My Wild West was known as America's "National Entertainment." My headquarters were located in a tent community just east of the Rockies. Every morning I watched the United States flag being raised by the sole survivor of Custer's massacre, the old soldier, and it made my heart beat just a little faster.

My staff consisted of Nate Salsbury, my efficient producer and director, Major "Arizona" John Burke, my prolix publicist, Ed Goodman, my nephew and corporate secretary, Col. Prentiss Ingraham, the most prolific Buffalo Bill dime novelist who ever lived, and Jules Keen, the Wild West's treasurer and accountant. Together we ran a show that was more dependable than the Pony Express, which at one time I rode for and set several distance-speed records.

Buffalo Bill's Wild West boasted the top acts of the day. We had Annie Oakley, the world's most famous woman marksman, and her husband-manager, Frank Butler. Then there was Munoz and Manuel the Mexican whip and fast-draw act, the dynamic Duce duo, daredevil cowboy trick riders, and of course Buck Taylor, King of the Cowboys, not to mention the Deadwood Stage, Buffalo Bill's Cowboy Band, plus hundreds of brave cowboys and fierce Indians.

At this time in my life I had no problems. Oh, there was Ned Buntline, who hung around the Buffalo Bar trying to destroy the legends about me he helped to create. He'd sit in there by the hour telling stories to Crutch and any of the cowhands who stopped by, but these people were too devoted to truly listen, let alone believe! Then, of course, there was Chief Sitting Bull, who joined my show in 1885 because he was more comfortable with me than rotting in the Standing Rock Indian Jail. Now, I'd heard all about Bull's feats as battling Chief of the Hunkpapa Sioux, but when he arrived at my show with McLaughlin, the Indian agent, I had doubts if his act would ever work. He brought William Halsey his interpreter with him, and some say he was the one with all the brains.

No matter what I did to try to improve the Chief's act, he was bent on frustrating me at every turn. He said he only joined my show to meet the "Great Father," President of the US of A, Grover Cleveland, but I knew inside he wanted to be with me in the show business more than anything else. If that wasn't true, Bull'd never have become Chief.

Being a man of culture and of arts, I enjoyed the finest things. All my favorite women were great opera singers. I had close associations with Margaret, a talented mezzo contralto, Lucille Du Charmes, an enjoyable lyric coloratura, and Nina Cavalini, a tintilating soprano. Unfortunately, these women all knew how to hold their breath better than holding their man, and had to be replaced.

In the arena, Buffalo Bill's Wild West had no peer. My arenic director Johnny Baker and his top wrangler Osborne Dart staged the best action in the business. And, of course, there I was, coming to the rescue whenever it was necessary. Chief Sitting Bull's act was a bit less exciting. Matter of fact, it was plain dull. But the fans were satisfied at just taking a gander at the bloodthirsty savage, and I had to let it go at that.

But I had problems with that Indian. He managed to turn Annie against me. He even tried to escape. But part of being the Lion of the Show Business was knowing just when to roar, and I certainly did know that. Nate Salsbury was a great help dealing with the Indians. So was Burke. They had more patience with them. But I paid my Indians top wages and they loved me for it. And I attracted royalty and great people, and they loved me, too.

Grover Cleveland and his wife Frances Folsom actually did make their way to my Wild West. It was on the night of their honeymoon. Nate and I staged the first night show of our history, and it was spectacular. Afterwards, Nate arranged a gala celebration in the Mayflower, where my personal offices and quarters were. It was a magnificent evening, marred only by Bull and Halsey's interruption, but the President handled them. It was on that very night I decided to visit Ned Buntline. He was alone in the bar with Crutch. I'll never forget that encounter. Ned tried to insult me. Said it was the thrill of his life to have invented me. Well, I wouldn't stand for that kind of abuse and in no time he was out of my camp. Gone. Leaving me alone.

After that time, I went through a period of unrest.

3

Times were changing. Nate was on the road more, preparing our visits to Europe and such. I even had a dream, which is rare for me seeing's how I don't dream. But I dreamt that Sitting Bull came to the Mayflower. I dreamed that I told him the truth. I faced that man and said that in one hundred years, in other people's shows, I would still be Buffalo Bill, star! And he'd still be the Indian. I never saw him again.

Word of Sitting Bull's death at Standing Rock by Indian police reached my village during an afternoon performance. I was in the arena at the time. I'm not sure to this day who told me. Or what my reaction was.

In the American West a hundred years ago, certain elements of life were impervious to change, while other elements were the essence of change. Somewhere between these extremes was the voice of experience.

An old soldier raises the flag over a crude log fort. In the distance, the Rocky Mountains form a backdrop for the flag and the fort. A bugle plays.

Some distance away in the shadow of that rugged range, a weary western settler leads his workhorse home from a field. The settler's child rides atop the harnessed horse. The settler's humble cabin is some distance away.

An old man's voice, thick with age and whiskey, comments. It is the old soldier speaking.

4

Ladies and gentlemen, your attention, please. What you are about to experience is not a show for entertainment. It is a review of the down-to-earth events that made the American frontier. In less than fifteen years this great nation will celebrate the twentieth century. We do not know what glories await us in the future, but we do know of our past that laid the foundation. And this foundation was not built from heroes. But from the anonymous settler. His house was but a shack roofed-in with sod. Ofttimes the floor was made of clay. One door shut out the wind and storm. One window greeted the dawning day. These brave souls survived not only nature but the savage instincts of man, paving the way for the heroes that endured. Welcome then to the real events enacted by men and women of the American frontier, to whose courage, strength and, above all, faith, this piece of our history is dedicated.

The settler and child are very near home when war whoops are heard. Indians appear. They attack the settler and circle the cabin. The settler's wife and boy are killed trying to flee. The child on horseback is killed, and then the father. The last child, a girl, is captured and tossed across a painted pony. The Indians suffer a single casualty. A young brave circling the cabin rides into a clothesline and is trampled when he falls.

Life was hard in the old West . . . and it was often surprising. As now we are surprised to hear a voice shouting.

5

Cease the action!

Indians return to the cabin, laughing and talking. The captive girl slides down from the horse. A dozen men rush into view. They are led by a small man in a bright yellow raincoat. He is carrying a megaphone, and shouting comments. The brisk bantam in the yellow slicker is Nate Salsbury, producer and prime mover of BUFFALO BILL'S WILD WEST.

SALSBURY
Isabel, is that your wardrobe? You look just like the dirt.

The settler's wife rises from the dead now and walks away from the others. The settler and the dead childred come alive also and dust themselves off.

Salsbury's entourage includes a young man smaller even than Nate himself. He is Johnny Baker, arenic director of the WILD WEST. Then there is a black cowhand named Osborne Dart, and a giant cowboy in a bearskin coat, who is Buck Taylor, "King of the Cowboys," star performer in the WILD WEST. Buck bullies everyone in sight, especially Osborne Dart and and Johnny Baker.

There are others. Prop men, wranglers, costumers . . . the sort of people that are needed to create such a show as this.

And by now we are aware that what we have been watching is not a real massacre but a rehearsal massacre for the show . . . BUFFALO BILL'S WILD WEST SHOW.

JOHNNY

Let's have some screams when the Indians are attacking. We need lots of screams.
(*calls to Salsbury*)
Do you want to run it again?

Osborne Dart bends over the fallen brave who was thrown from his mount by the clothesline.

DART

Mr. Salsbury! Mr. Salsbury! He's been hurt. Oh, my God. A horse stepped clean through him. Buck! Get your foot off of him.

SALSBURY

Buck! Somebody get Eats Rabbit to the dispensary.

JOHNNY

It ain't Eats Rabbit. It's Brown Horse.

SALSBURY

I don't care who it is. Just get him to the dispensary.

Rehearsal is over. A team of horses is hitched to the settler's cabin and drags it away. The prop men take down the clothesline and a fake tree. Salsbury and his group walk away. They dodge a racing stagecoach which is being chased by a gang of outlaws. Apparently, WILD WEST acts are rehearsing all over over the place.

JOHNNY

I was thinking. What if we had fire and burned the cabin down?

SALSBURY

We'll keep the clothesline in but have them ride around it.

JOHNNY

Do you think it would help if we had fire, have the cabin on fire?

Among Salsbury's affectations is a taste of neologisms of his own invention.

SALSBURY

Fire! What an extraordinable idea. We'll have a flaming arrow come right into the settler's cabin. Then we'll have it all ignite. You can talk to special inventions about that.

Salsbury keeps walking briskly.

SALSBURY

You know what we're doing here? We're involved in living American drama. I mean, we're trying to show things as they really were beyond the Missouri. So you can't have anything that isn't authentic, genuine, and real. There will be nothing fake about us. Nothing gimcrack about this show.

Salsbury and group walk through a gate and step onto a wooden sidewalk. They are not in the wilderness after all. There is a village here, a complete town of tents and wooden structures.

There is a laundry tent, a telegraph office, a dry goods store, a curio shop, a harness and Saddlery repair and much more, lining a single main street.

The old Fort glimpsed at the beginning is part of this town.

Brown Horse's body is carried to the camp dispensary for repairs. The dispensary tent also houses a barber shop and a bar.

On the main street between the Saddlery and the Band tent, where Buffalo Bill's Cowboy Band is rehearsing, is Annie Oakley's shooting range.

Annie is shooting a rifle with her left hand. Her right is in a sling. Annie's tall, dark and handsome husband, Frank Butler, assists her. He holds a small hand mirror so she can see behind her. She is not facing the target but shooting over her shoulder.

> BUTLER
> Ready. Let 'er go!

> ANNIE
> Steady.

> BUTLER
> Steady as a rock.

She fires a round and breaks a bottle.

> BUTLER
> There you go. Wait till Nate sees this!

Annie narrows her eyes and aims for a second bottle.

By the wooden Fort, the old soldier rehearses a speech. His audience is a group of Indian children.

We were outnumbered five to one and I knew the only hope was to kill the war chief. So I snuck out into the bushes. I found the Cheyenne camp and with a bullet from this very rifle at over four hundred yards, I shot and killed that chief. Two years later at a church service in Deadwood City, I met and rubbed elbows with a young man named William F. Cody . . .

Salsbury is at Annie's rifle range. He watches her shoot with her left hand. She fires a round and another bottle breaks.

SALSBURY

Ah! Just like the old missy.

Salsbury walks on and Butler quickly hands his mirror to an Indian boy.

BUTLER

Nate. Hold on for a second.
(*to Indian boy*)
Do whatever missy tells you.
(*rushes after Salsbury*)
I'll be back in a second, darlin'. Nate, I want you to back me up in this against Bill.

Salsbury talks to the band director, who is standing in his path.

SALSBURY

Sweeney. The Indian music on the settlers' cabin is the wrong ethnic. It's too Ukranian. Johnny, get over here.

It's Buntline. I want to protect Annie from those low-grade dime novels he writes. She's been suffering a lot lately, with her bum arm and all.

SALSBURY
Frank, one thing is for certain, that nobody in this camp has more affection or perspect for Miss Annie Oakley than Nate Salsbury. And it was never my disquest for her to do that ride and risk her limb.

They pass the first (now stuffed) buffalo that Bill Cody killed at age eleven.

SALSBURY
Why is this dirty? Do you know that every day I have to come out here and talk to you about cleaning this buffalo?

BUTLER
Nate, are you listening to anything I say?

Salsbury and Butler are approaching the only grand structure on the street. The Mayflower is headquarters for the WILD WEST. It is a huge tent with a colorful wooden front which features a large mural of a dashing man on a prancing stallion. The man is, of course, the Honorable William F. Cody, "Buffalo Bill." The Mayflower is his office and his home.

The interior of the Mayflower is spacious. There is a central meeting room with a long table. There are momentos of Buffalo Bill everywhere. At the long table sits Prentiss Ingraham, a cavalier dime novelist, who is telling a story of great personal bravery to Ed Goodman, Cody's gossipy nephew. Also present is Jules Keen, the nervous accountant.

PRENTISS

Nevertheless, Ed, a Spanish soldier's attacking me, his eyes flashing fire and ferocity . . . He lunges, I block. He lunges. I block. Two of his compadres capture me from behind. I'm prisoner again.

ED

Tell me. How'd they poke out your eye?

PRENTISS

That's how. Anything you want to tell me about your Uncle Will, Ed?

Two cowboys (August and Trotter) enter.

AUGUST

Excuse me, Mr. Keen. We have an appointment with Mr. Salsbury.

KEEN

He's practicing the settlers' cabin act in the practice area.

ED

(rising)
Can I help you gents?

AUGUST

We have an appointment with Mr. Salsbury.

ED

He isn't here right now.

12

He's coming down the street right now.

Salsbury's and Butler's entrance increases the volume.

BUTLER

. . . Nate, we gotta make him see what a serious situation this is . . .

Salsbury does his best to ignore Butler. He goes to his cluttered desk.

SALSBURY

(to Keen)
What is this . . . I've seen more organization when I was an actor in stock . . .

BUTLER

Would you please listen to me? We happen to be having a conversation about Annie Oakley. I'm her husband and I have a duty to protect her from . . .

Salsbury picks up a cable from his desk.

SALSBURY

What is this? Anybody know about this? When did this transmit come in?

BUTLER

Nate, you're not listening to me and I'm getting mad.

SALSBURY

Prentiss, I'm late. I'm sorry.

BUTLER

Nate, I'm not asking anymore. I want you to get Bill's assurance that every word written about her ...

SALSBURY

Ed, these are things we must go over today. Where are those three names I gave you today?

Ed gets his notebook from his desk.

BUTLER

... Must have truth, decency and honesty ...

Prentiss copies Butler's words in his notebook. Prentiss is always looking for material for his adventure novels, his half-dimes as they are called.

PRENTISS

(*to himself*)
... Truth, decency, honesty ...

BUTLER

And that means no Buntline. Damn it, Nate, you're not listening to me. Are you gonna tell Bill or not?

SALSBURY

(*to Ed*)
The Cody Cavalcade is not commercable enough.

He turns to Butler finally.

SALSBURY

Frank. Why don't you tell him yourself?

BUTLER
All right, damn it, I will.

Butler heads for Cody's office. Ed rushes to stop him.

ED
Mr. Butler, he's with Major Burke. He said he didn't want to be interrupted.

BUTLER
Yeah, well, this is damn important.

He disappears through doorway. The cowboys meanwhile are complaining to Salsbury at his desk.

AUGUST
We don't want to be Mexicans.

SALSBURY
What do you want to be?

AUGUST
We're from Australia. We want to be Tasmanians.

From behind the leather curtain separating Cody's office can be heard Cody's and Burke's voices.

CODY'S VOICE
Frank, good to see you. My glass got empty somehow. Could you go to the bar and get me a couple of fingers, please?

BURKE'S VOICE
Yes. I'd like a fistful of that medicine myself, Frank.

15

Frank reappears with two empty mugs. He looks chagrined.

> SALSBURY
> (to cowboys)
> We're not in the Tasmanian business.

> TROTTER
> But what about our blue eyes?

> SALSBURY
> I didn't hire you for your eyes. I hired you for your whip and you for your gun. Now I'm gonna give you almost a top spot in the show. Right after cowboy fun. You are going to be Manuel and Munoz. Los Latigos Mexicanos.

Butler crosses back from the bar to Cody's office again.

Ed and Prentiss have taken seats by the leather room divider to eavesdrop on Cody's conversation.

> BUTLER'S VOICE
> Now, Bill, I have something very important to talk to you about . . .

> CODY'S VOICE
> Thank you, Frank. Now would you mind getting out of the middle of my conference? Ed, I said no interruptions. Honor my wishes.

> ED
> Yes, sir, but . . .

> CODY
> No buts. I said honor my wishes!

16

Butler leaves the Mayflower in direct honor of Cody's wishes. Ed and Prentiss continue to eavesdrop so that they may be more aware of Cody's wishes.

> CODY'S VOICE
>
> Pardner, if you hit the target we could revolutionize the show business. Not to mention Injun relations.

> BURKE'S VOICE
>
> I'll be firm.

> CODY'S VOICE
>
> That's right. Hell, the only difference between Injuns and whites in a situation like this is whites already know how it's gonna come out.

> BURKE'S VOICE
>
> I'm glad we thought of it. It's a great idea. You gonna hold at forty dollars a week?

> CODY'S VOICE
>
> Like a rock. Not a red cent more.

About this time more music invades the WILD WEST. This time the lyrical voice of a mezzo-contralto tracing the melody of an operatic aria.

> BURKE'S VOICE
>
> Suppose he holds out for more?

> CODY'S VOICE
>
> Huh? Oh. Offer him forty . . . And if he holds out, give him . . . fifty.

BURKE'S VOICE
You're a fox, Bill.

CODY'S VOICE
You get going, Major. I got things to do.

BURKE'S VOICE
Bill, the Army's gonna want us to play politics.

CODY'S VOICE
Hell, we *are* playing politics. They want him in the show as much as we do.

BURKE'S VOICE
Wish me luck, Bill.

CODY'S VOICE
You don't need luck, you got me. Remember, fifty bucks tops, and I got all photographic and souvenir rights. Everything historical is mine.

BURKE'S VOICE
Everything historical is yours, Bill.

Salsbury, who knows everyone's secrets already, reads a review of his WILD WEST SHOW.

SALSBURY
(*reading*)
"Buffalo Bill's Wild West came to St. Louis and the result was nothing short of disaster. Despite overblown reviews by eastern critics, Buffalo Bill's Wild West can only be described

as a sham. Producer Nate Salsbury bills the indulgent theatrics as America's National Entertainment, but America's National Charade is a more appropriate description. The action is stagey and garish, the animals dumb and slow, perhaps drugged . . ." Drugged? That's probably libelous . . . "The costumes are false and resemble leftovers from Cody and Salsbury's earlier debacles onstage." Who the hell is Huntsey Whitoh?

KEEN

Huntsey Whitoh? Never heard of him.

The sensual sound of the opera singer who lives in Cody's bedroom has only one meaning in the Mayflower, and everyone on the staff clears out when that mating call is heard.

Burke comes from Cody's office. He has a grand manner. He is publicist for the WILD WEST and an old crony of Cody's. He is dressed for travel.

ED

Does he want to see me, Major Burke?

BURKE

Doesn't sound like he wants to see anybody in this room.

SALSBURY

Burke, who in Hades is this Huntsey Whitoh?

BURKE

Huntsey Whitoh. Gossip columnist. St. Louis Dispatch.

. . . St. Louis Dispatch.

ED

I didn't know we was in the St. Louis Dispatch. Is my name there?

KEEN

(*wryly*)
Of course, Eddie. At the bottom.

SALSBURY

This could do us a lot of rhetorical injury. Other papers could lift this off.

There is a rivalry between Burke and Salsbury, a natural tension of two courtiers closest to the king.

BURKE

(*smiling*)
We'll have to have some metaphorical medicine. Spirits of Hyperbole, perhaps. You mustn't take umbrage at that flatulent palaver. My God, as an actor I suffered a wagonload of brickbats . . . I learned to ignore them.

Salsbury follows Burke and the others to the door.

BURKE

You're an old troubadour, Nate.

SALSBURY

I'm not in the troubadour business anymore, Burke. I'm in the stage picture business. And remember Bill and I are holding at forty!

> BURKE

Rest, rest, perturbed spirit.

Outside, Ed and Jules head down the main street.

Prentiss watches Burke load his buggy.

> BURKE

It's a long ride to Standing Rock and I have a lively imagination. By the time I return, I shall have a hundred tales of cheer. Whoa, boy.

> PRENTISS

Going by way of the dispensary, Major?

> BURKE

Yes, get in. Get up, boy.

> PRENTISS

Major?

> BURKE

Yes?

> PRENTISS
> *(reading from his notes)*

"Bull's-eye. Heroic villains. Revolutionize. Injuns. Whites . . ."

> BURKE

Say. Sounds like you've got all the elements of a first-rate half-dime.

> PRENTISS

What's the plot, Major?

BURKE
(halting buggy in front of dispensary)

The plot. The plot. Well, you're an author. What is the plot? I'll tell you. You string those pearls together and you'll have a first-rate Buffalo Bill story. And let me read it when you get back. I'll even give you the legend. Enemies in 75. Friends in 86.

PRENTISS

(climbing out)

Godspeed.

Burke is off. Prentiss enters the dispensary. Cowboys, wranglers and performers line the bar. Prentiss finds a spot and orders a beer. In a moment he is joined by Jules Keen.

At a table not far from Prentiss and Keen, Ned Buntline holds court to a bunch of cowhands. Ned is a middle-aged novelist and adventurer who had much to do in creating the legend that is Buffalo Bill.

BUNTLINE

In '68 I go west searching for a new frontier hero to write about. I read accounts of the battle of Summit Springs and want to meet the champion of that conflict, Major Frank North, but the Major is averse to publicity and refuses to talk. So one morning I'm wandering around camp and I see this scrawny kid sleeping under a wagon. I drag him out. I take one look and I know I can make him a star. I ask his name, says Cody, Bill Cody, I says what do ya do, says he's a scout and buffalo hunter. Well, I'm eager to write about somebody 'cause I got a batch of excitin' plots

22

I might take to Hickock but I'm mad at him,
so I tell the kid from now his name is Buffalo
Bill and in six months the whole country's
gonna know about you. That's all I say and I
walk away. Sure enough, these stories come
out and are a big success and the kid comes
lookin' for me, scared to death about the
legends I created but real excited with his new
fame. Again I say only one thing. I say,
"Buffalo Bill, any youngster like yourself who
figures he's gonna set the world on fire best
not forget where he got the matches . . ."

He strikes a wooden match and lights his pipe.

Buntline spots Prentiss at the Bar.

BUNTLINE
Ah, Shakespeare of the half-dimes. Have a
seat.

Prentiss joins Buntline at his table. Jules hovers
behind.

PRENTISS
Something's up, Ned. Bill and Nate sent
Burke outta here on the fly.

BUNTLINE
Got any ideas?

PRENTISS
Burke gave me a few clues . . . something
about Injuns and whites, heroic villain, fifty
bucks a week and . . . foes in '75, friends in
'86.

That shouldn't be hard to figure. Bill and
Nate are in the big time. They can afford to
spend fifty dollars a week. Now tell me what
Injun villain is worth that much? Sitting Bull,
of course.

JULES AND PRENTISS

Sittin' Bull?

JULES

Is he tame?

PRENTISS

What about the army?

BUNTLINE

The army'll love it. They can't shoot him. Not
till they get those Sioux treaties signed. So
they put him in a Wild West Show. Make a
broad-assed fool outta him, and the rest is
easy. A rock ain't a rock once it's gravel. Get
it?

JULES

They're gonna stone him?

PRENTISS

Shh. I'll explain later, Jules. And the army
triumphs again. Thanks for the solution, Ned.
I'll do the same for you sometime.

Jules Keen and Prentiss come out of the dispensary.

KEEN

I don't know what he meant by that rock and
gravel line.

PRENTISS

It's simply Buntline's way of saying that he lost his power, He's tame.

KEEN

You're not gonna write that down? I don't think that's so memorable.

Ed crosses their path.

ED

Mr. Keen, I hear the new act is General Custer's brother.

KEEN

That's not what we hear, Eddie.

ED

Well, who is it then?

PRENTISS

Sitting Bull.

ED

Sittin' Bull?

PRENTISS

Sittin' Bull.

ED

Sittin' Bull. I didn't know he was interested in the show business.

PRENTISS

If he wasn't interested in the show business he would never have become chief.

Keen and Prentiss walk on toward the Mayflower. One of the Duce girls races past Ed riding upside-down on her palomino. The Duce girls are fancy trick riders who earlier played the part of the settler's children in the Indian attack on the settler's cabin.

ED

Hi, Joy.
   (*he ponders*)
Sittin' Bull! I tell you there ain't no business like the show business.

It is nighttime, and the determinedly mournful sound of Indian chanting drifts from a field behind the dispensary where Buffalo Bill's "Authentic" Indian Village is set up. The village consists of a couple dozen canvas teepees gaily decorated in the bold yellow and red colors of the WILD WEST. On performance days, the tourists pay a nickel each to browse through the ersatz encampment where Buffalo Bill's tamed savages reside.

This night, however, there is no performance. There are no tourists. The goings-on tonight are strictly real. Brown Horse, the young brave who was trampled in the morning's rehearsal, is dying. The Indians sing for his spirit.

At the other end of the camp, in the big Mayflower structure, a woman sings an aria, in Italian. Her voice is strong as the wind across the prairie.

The singer, Margaret, glides through the empty, lamplit meeting room of the Mayflower clutching a gigantic two-handled glass mug to her bosom. She sings her way to an ornate bar and there she fills

the outsized schooner with whiskey. Her aria be-
comes a paean to her hero and lover.

MARGARET

> (*singing*)
> Buffalo Bill, Buffalo Bill, Buffalo ... Billie ...

Margaret strolls back across the room in the direction of Cody's quarters. On the way, she passes the
large oil painting of Cody astride his rampant white
stallion, Brigham. She lifts the schooner slightly to
salute him. Her voice rises to the occasion.

The image of Cody is magnificent. It is one to hold
our eye for some time. And so it does, as Margaret
glides away to Cody's room.

Nate Salsbury's resonant voice welcomes us to day-
time and another show rehearsal. This time there
are many acts working simultaneously in the big
performance arena not far from the Indian village.

An improved version of the "Attack on the Settler's
Cabin" takes up the center of the ring. Salsbury
stands on a platform by the entrance. The little man
is nearly invisible behind a podium and a huge,
triple-horned, brass megaphone which spreads his
voice to the empty stands.

Johnny Baker stands beside him taking notes and
keeping an eye on every activity.

SALSBURY

> As America's national bird spread her wings
> and flew across these states united, she saw
> her offspring moving westward, settling, carv-
> ing the frontier life amidst hardship, against

untamed savages, and in the bitter cold . . . and what you are watching now, good people, is no sham, no act, no cheap circus, but the exact representation of early pioneer life beyond the Missouri . . . as performed by real Indians astride real horses attacking real Americans!

Whooping Indians again attack the weary settler and again they slaughter his unfortunate family.

In another part of the arena, Annie Oakley fires at a gold coin that Frank Butler holds between his fingers. Young Ed Goodman stands behind her. His chatter puts her concentration to the test.

ED
Sure, I'd like to take a wife, but first I have to find a girl. One that's as pure as the Lord describes.

ANNIE
Sure.

ED
And for some reason, that's hard to find around this business.

ANNIE
Oh, Ed. It just isn't so.

ED
(looking at laundry mistresses in stands)
See those girls over there? See that little girl on the end? The one that works in the laundry?

ANNIE

Little Joyce?

ED

Don't point. I saw her huggin' a man between the tents last night.

ANNIE

Well, that's nice.

ED

But he was a married man.

ANNIE

Oh, Ed, you're dreaming.

Prentiss Ingraham is seen with a well-dressed group of visitors, highlighted by the arresting beauty of Madame Lucille Du Charmes, another opera singer.

In the arena, things look bleak for the brave settler and his family. They have been murdered by the untamed savages and their daughter has been tied to a totem pole, which incidentally is the second part of the WILD WEST's first two-part presentation.

SALSBURY

Ladies and gentlemen . . . a tragic . . . but true portraytment. Tragic, yes, but a situation not beyond repair and avenge! Ladies and gentlemen, you can lower your handkerchiefs and raise your flags, for, behold, here is the man you've all been waiting for . . . The man whose place in history and solid character have made him popular throughout the continent. Ladies and gentlemen, the one, the only . . . *America's national entertainer* . . . so put it all together now for William F. Cody . . . BUFFALO BILL!

And there he is, on the white horse just like in his portrait. Better than the portrait, for no artist of infinite skill could recapture men's dreams. The Indians flee from the man as if his mere presence is the only necessary deterrent. Then, with customary style and grace, Buffalo Bill Cody rides to Madame Du Charmes, dismounts and kisses her hand. On the podium, Johnny Baker calls through the tripliphone.

JOHNNY
Everyone to the podium, on the triple.

PRENTISS
Mademoiselle Du Charmes . . . Je vous presente . . . I would like to present the legendary Buffalo Bill.

CODY
Welcome to Buffalo Bill's Wild West.

LUCILLE
I'm pleased to meet you, Mr. Bill. What a beautiful horse.

CODY
Yes. Nice mouth. Bright, too. You notice he's ridden in the style of the Grenadier Guard in preparation for my visit with the Queen next fall.

The man next to Lucille offers Cody his hand.

30

DWIGHT

Dwight Frye. Miss Du Charmes's press agent. We have just had a great success with Handel's "Renaldo" in San Francisco.

CODY

Delightful music.

And Lucille sings a few bars.

CODY

A coloratura, huh?

LUCILLE

A lyrico spinto coloratura!

Ed appears with a stack of mail.

ED

Uncle Will, here's a transmit from Major Burke.

Cody takes the telegram. He has been staring into Lucille's eyes. He kisses her hand again.

CODY

From Denver, eh?

He walks away. Ed follows. Annie is shooting nearby. The entire company is at the podium.

SALSBURY

Is everybody here? Joy Duce, Greg, special inventions? After our last rehearsal, both Buffalo Bill and myself had our reservements about the new show. You know, perhaps we'd

bitten off more than was chewable. That by
enlarging the show we had dissimproved it.
But after what I've just seen, I'm positive
we're all doing the right thing.

Annie shoots coins from Frank Butler's fingers.

CODY
That's very stylish, Missy.

Cody walks on, reading the telegram Ed has given
him. His eyes light up. Frank Butler calls for him
just as Annie fires a shot that scares Ed and sends
him crashing into his uncle.

BUTLER
Bill, Buntline's in camp. And I know that
you'll be upset if he writes anything to harm
our precious Annie.

CODY
(to Ed)
Did you hear that? Why didn't you tell me
that?

ED
I did, sir. Three nights ago.

CODY
Three nights ago! Oh . . .
(he calls loud)
Nate!

Salsbury appears.

CODY
Frank tells me that Buntline is in camp.

32

SALSBURY

Yes. I know. He's back at his old table, but just say the word and I'll have him removed from the lot.

CODY

No, Buntline and I go back too far for that. You get rid of him and just don't tell me that I told you to do it.

Cody, Salsbury and Ed leave the arena. Cody spots some Indians huddled in the nearby Indian village.

CODY

What's going on over there?

SALSBURY

They're burying Brown Horse. He got killed in rehearsal.

CODY

You never told me that.

SALSBURY

Yes, I did. Three days ago.

CODY

Oh. Brown Horse was Shoshone, wasn't he? I won the medal of honor for killing every member of a Shoshone raiding party in '72. Don't seem that long ago.

ED

You rode into the valley of death and you rode out again.

33

CODY
(*looking at the burial site*)
Remember, son, the last thing a man wants to
do is the last thing he does!

Ed ponders that as Cody and Salsbury walk toward
Main Street.

CODY
That was a good idea you had.

SALSBURY
What's that?

CODY
To give the Indians slower horses. Read this.

SALSBURY
(*excited about telegram*)
At-a-way, Pard.

CODY
Money in the bank.

Cody gestures toward bar.

CODY
Oh. Don't forget to tell him like I said . . .

SALSBURY
Right. And I won't tell you.

In the bar, Crutch is counting money. Buntline is
in the barber shop shaving.

CRUTCH
Business is good. Gettin' better.

BUNTLINE

That's because times are bad. Getting worse. That's when the show business flourishes, when times are bad.

CRUTCH

Hope it stays that way.

Salsbury walks in the back door of the bar to be alone with Buntline.

BUNTLINE

Well, I'll be goddamned if it ain't Nervous Nate.

SALSBURY

Buntline, you're not doing anybody a favor by being here.

BUNTLINE

I ain't in the favor business, Nate.

SALSBURY

I want you to leave my camp, now!

BUNTLINE

And it surely is your camp, ain't it, Nate? And you're doing a great job, too. Much better than I coulda ever done. Organized. Profitable. Sober. You're a man's man, Nate. A producer's producer.

SALSBURY

Don't patronize me, Buntline. I mean what I say.

I know you do, Nate. That's your reputation.
Nate Salsbury means what he says. And what
a fine citizen you made of Bill. Don't even
seem like the same man. Never gets in trouble, never looks bad in public.

SALSBURY

All I care about is the Wild West. I am going
to Codyfy the world.

BUNTLINE

(*sarcastic*)
Now why didn't I think of that?

SALSBURY

Because I'm the only partner Bill Cody ever
had who tells him the truth. And in the end
we always agree.

BUNTLINE

I was taught when two partners *always* agree,
one of 'em ain't necessary.

SALSBURY

Look, Buntline, nothing personal. It's just
that you're part of the past and we're simply
not in the yesterday business. We've just
signed the most futurable act in our history
and I won't have anything or anybody creating problems.

BUNTLINE

Who's the act?

SALSBURY

(*proud; holding telegram*)
Sitting Bull.

(*feign surprise*)
Sitting Bull, no kidding! Well, Nate, that's quite a coup. But I ain't leavin' here till Bill Cody comes in and personally *invites* me out!

It's night again. Cody is slumped at a table in his bedroom, having read a depressing letter. Margaret lies on the bed behind him.

CODY
Finish this for me, will ya, Margaret?

MARGARET
What is it, sweetie?

CODY
My eyes water up when I read words like that from my own wife.

Margaret gets off the bed, hugs him.

MARGARET
Sure, I will. Put your head down. Good boy.

She reads the letter while perched on his lap.

MARGARET
"And I know you are as unfaithful to me as a stray dog, and just about as inhuman. Your financial treatment of me has been totally unfair and rude, so I am buying land with my own savings to be protected from your heartless dealings. I am also certain that I get title to the gold mine, though in all these years you or it have never paid off. Hoping I never lay

37

eyes on you again, I remain your sorrowful wife, Lulu."

CODY

Gold mine, huh? How'd she find out about that? Remind me to write my lawyers in the morning.
(*continuing*)
I want you to read something I'm sending to Sister.

MARGARET

Why do I have to read these silly letters you write your sister, Bill?

CODY

Why do you have to read these silly letters? 'Cause I'm the Lion of the Show Business, and I got something to say.

She takes the letter. Cody walks to a mirror. He begins to do something with his hair. What Cody does with his hair might to this day be regarded as a *terrifically* kept secret. He is wearing a wig.

MARGARET

(*reading*)
"Dear Sister, your good letter received but I was disappointed to find no gossip about anything. Eddie is doing real well and going to church each and every Sunday and you will see by my last picture that I am lighter than I have been in years but my energy is greater and this is because I kept my promise to Nate Salsbury and quit drinking altogether and find I don't miss it a bit . . ."

38

Margaret pauses to catch her breath, and to give Cody a doubtful eye about the drinking.

> CODY

Go ahead.

He preens while she reads.

> MARGARET

"These are fine times for me 'cause there ain't a person on earth I'd trade places with as I am one of the most respected men in the frontier and in arts."

> CODY
> (*still at mirror*)

Someday my hair is gonna be as long as Custer's ... was.

> MARGARET

"Strangers know my name, but however I don't find I learn much from anybody but I am always polite and forgive our differences like the professional American I truly am ... Here is a poem somebody in camp wrote ... 'Nature's proud she made this man, This man, Buffalo Bill. For it's always been his plan To save others from the kill ...' "

Cody takes the letter from her.

> CODY

Here. Let me have a crack at that.

He reads it aloud with the proper emphasis.

" 'Nature's proud she made this man—
This man, Buffalo Bill.
For it's always been his plan
To Save others from the kill.

So during hard time years
He dries orphans' tears
And relieves widows' fears.
Don't you, Bill?
Often lightening hearts of lead—
This smiling Bill.

When Sitting Bull rides to camp
Searching for Longhair Bill,
He knows he'll meet the champ
Of courage and iron will.

Before ten thousand fans,
Each will take their stand.
A future challenge delivers one man—
Our own, Buffalo Bill.

He's a brother, that you know—
Generous Bill.
And none of us is white as snow.
Are we, Bill?

But if Red men come to fight,
Let's show 'em all our might—
Including being right.
Carry on, Bill.

So when Judgment Day shall come,
And you know it will,
It won't be makeup on
Authentic Bill.

You'll be in your tallest boots,
Among chips and cattle chutes,
Still sending down your roots,
From up there, Bill.' ”

As Cody reads this poem, accented by Margaret's
version of "Greensleeves," we find a portrait of
Cody hanging above the piano. A long close look reveals activity from within the man's face, as if riders
were coming toward us out of Cody's eyes.

Cody's face gradually disappears and we see Burke,
returning with Sitting Bull, coming over the horizon
with a retinue of calvary and a number of Indians.
As they approach the camp, one can make out a
giant male Indian in a red blanket, and a small old
man riding beside him. Several braves and squaws
complete the entourage.

From the top of the Fort, Prentiss is looking through
the telescope. Ed is asking Jules about scalps while
Nate makes notes for his opening remarks to Sitting
Bull.

SALSBURY
Ed, did you arrange for Sweeney about the
welcoming music? He's starting with piece
number four, right?

ED
Yes, and I also told him to have number two
ready in case you change your mind.

SALSBURY
Double guessing me, son . . . that's good.

Ed smiles.

41

Now, stop worrying and see if you can't help your Uncle Bill . . .

Yes, sir.

Ed leaves, as Prentiss steps up to Nate and Jules takes the telescope.

PRENTISS

Looks like John will ride to the top of the list with this one, Nate. "Major Burke's Greatest Coup."

SALSBURY

You'll never hear Nate Salsbury deny that John Burke isn't the limit, but he publicates himself at the show's expense. And that's rank.

PRENTISS

Of all those words, only two will be remembered . . . "Buffalo Bill."

Ed Goodman enters Cody's bedroom, looking for his uncle.

The shower is running. Ed pokes his head in, only to find Margaret showering. He quickly draws the shower curtain, then sees Cody sitting by the window looking with his telescope at Sitting Bull's arrival.

ED

Uncle Will, they're coming. You've only got a few minutes.

42

Cody continues to watch.

      Uncle Will...

Ed bends for a better look out the window. Margaret is singing in the shower.

ED

      He must be the one in the red blanket. He sure don't look like no ordinary Injun.

CODY

      I ain't buying no ordinary Injun. Go help Nate with the welcoming committee.

Ed turns to comply, and Cody snatches the whiskey schooner from him.

CODY

      Thank you, son.

Ed leaves. Cody goes to his dresser to touch up his beard. Margaret pokes her head out of the shower and sings him a verse of personalized opera. Cody returns to the window carrying a fancy vest.

CODY

      (*looking out*)
      He didn't even dress up. Hell.

Crutch watches Sitting Bull's arrival from the doorway of the bar. Buntline is calm inside the bar.

BARTENDER

      Jesus H. Christ. Mr. Buntline, come here and look at Sitting Bull. That Injun's seven feet tall.

43

Buntline walks to the door and stands beside Crutch for a look at the Indians.

> BUNTLINE
> He's getting smaller every year.

Salsbury heads down Main Street to greet Burke.

> SALSBURY
> Buck, Johnny Baker, Dart. Come down here.

Salsbury speaks to the band leader.

> SALSBURY
> Sweeney. "Major Burke's Arrival," please.

He speaks to the photographer, Brewster.

> SALSBURY
> Do you have the right respective from there? I want this to be encompassing. Historical and encompassing.

Ed joins him.

> SALSBURY
> Where the hell's Bill?

> ED
> He'll be out.

> SALSBURY
> Has he been drinking?

> ED
> (defensive)
> Certainly not.

44

The camp has gathered, and all eyes are on the riders who dismount—except the older Indian who seems too weak to do so.

The civilians with Burke are Indian agents, Mc-Laughlin and Tompkins. The lieutenant is Ford, and his troopers flank the Indians.

> SALSBURY
>
> Splendid work, Burke. My compliments.

> BURKE
>
> It was a true test of the outer scales, but the game was worth the candle. Where's Bill?

> SALSBURY
>
> (*low*)
> Getting ready.

> BURKE
>
> (*equally low*)
> Getting ready for the big entrance, huh?

> SALSBURY
>
> So it seems. Were there any problems?

> BURKE
>
> You know how negotiations go. But it wasn't long until Sitting Bull realized that the sound of applause has a sweeter resonance than the clacking of rats' teeth.

McLaughlin and Tompkins step up. They are both miserable-looking creatures who've spent a lifetime beyond the reaches of soap and civilization.

45

MCLAUGHLIN

Major Burke, I'm ready to dispose of the prisoner.

BURKE

My sweet McLaughlin. You are now in Cody-land. I keep telling you, he is no longer a prisoner. He is a star in the Buffalo Bill heavens.

MCLAUGHLIN

Call him what you like, to me he's a murderer and he's in my custody till I turn him over to Cody.

BURKE

Nate, you should meet McLaughlin. He's an Indian agent out of Standing Rock.

Salsbury offers his hand to McLaughlin who ignores it.

SALSBURY

I'm Bill's partner. He'll be out momentably. I trust you had a pleasant trip.

MCLAUGHLIN

I had a miserable trip. I hate horsebackin' and I don't like delivering an Indian to a damn circus.

SALSBURY

One thing that Buffalo Bill's Wild West is not is a circus. Buffalo Bill will be out moment-ably but . . .

This delay doesn't set well with the United States government.

Don't be upset. Buffalo Bill's delayed entrance is part of his unerring sense of theatrical timing.

Just then Cody's fanfare is struck by the Buffalo Bill Cowboy Band. The Duce girls appear at the head of Main Street on their golden horses, carrying a banner with the name of "Buffalo Bill Cody" emblazoned on it.

Then Cody appears cantering under the banner on the magnificent white stallion, Brigham. We are all struck by the extraordinary image the man creates, as he rides down the street, saluting.

Cody arrives at the end of the street. He gestures, and the Duce girls whirl their horses, reversing the banner so that the legend on the opposite side can be read: "Chief Sitting Bull, Killer of Custer." The band changes to Indian drumbeats. Burke comes forward to shake Cody's hand. Everyone else is on foot now except Cody and the oldest Indian.

Hello, Bill. From the teeth of danger I have plucked the sweet rose of success.

Cody expands his greeting beyond Burke to the assembled crowd. His eyes rest firmly on the tall Indian.

CODY

Well, I'd just like to say . . . Congratulations on your arrival and a titanically monumentally welcome to Buffalo Bill's Wild West . . . Now me and my staff are the best at what we do, and what we do is make the best seem better. So when you hear what we got planned for you . . .

Just then the other Indian recognizes Annie Oakley. He waves at Annie and greets her in Sioux.

ANNIE

Hiya, Chief.

For the first time Cody and the others realize that Sitting Bull is not the tall, majestic Indian in the red blanket but the small, weary old man on the pinto. Cody does his best to continue, but he is clearly stunned that the little man is the legendary Sitting Bull.

CODY

. . . and you'll wonder why you didn't get into this business sooner.

The large Indian steps forward.

HALSEY

My name is William Halsey. Chief Sitting Bull has chosen to speak through me. The many moons of his incarceration have emptied his strength and he wishes to rest!

CODY

Oh. Halsey, huh? A white name. You got a little white blood in ya, Halsey?

48

The big Indian does not flinch at the chiding.

> **CODY**
>
> Halsey, you tell the chief that most of the people standing in front of him are members of the finest spectacle in the history of the show business. And I've watched each and every one of 'em grow from plain, raw talent to personages of importance. You tell your chief that we can do that for him, too. I guarantee he'll never be mistaken for a run-of-the-mill Injun chief after just one season with us, and most important, he'll have something to fall back on in his later years . . .

Just then Bull yawns. Cody mumbles.

> **CODY**
>
> A long trip, huh? Well, anyhow . . . I just wanna welcome you again into my show and into the show business itself. It ain't that much different than real life.

Crutch looks over the swinging doors of the bar as Cody rides up the street toward the Mayflower. Fly, a black cowboy who sweeps the bar, is beside Crutch.

> **CRUTCH**
>
> So the little fella's Sitting Bull. Hm. Doesn't look very savage to me. But I think I'll sleep with a shotgun anyway. The chief's famous for scalpin' folks in their beds.

Crutch goes inside and draws himself a beer. He takes a couple of boiled eggs from the backbar. Buntline is at his favorite table.

CRUTCH

(*to Fly*)
Get me some salt and pepper.
(*to Buntline*)
I sure hope Bill can handle him.

BUNTLINE

Reminds me of Bill's dealings with the Cheyenne at Republican River. Tall Bull was the war chief of the Cheyenne and when he was killed quite a few people took credit for doing it. Including Bill. Now some say that Bill ain't even in the village during the cavalry attack, and that he sneaks out and lets the Ninth fight it out without him. And others say he kills Tall Bull at four hundred yards with one shot. Well, the fact is they're *both* true. What happens is there's this terrific rain and hail storm as the cavalry begin their attack. Bill has a bad head cold and he figures he's done his duty by just finding the goddamn village, so he hightails it back in the direction of camp. Meanwhile, the cavalry attacks and Tall Bull escapes on his large bay and heads for the same hills where Bill's takin' a breather ...

CRUTCH

(*to Fly, who is sweeping*)
Hey, you missed some dirt. Right there. Sweep it up.

BUNTLINE

Now, Bill's drowning his lizard when he looks up across the ravine and spots this Injun atop the most beautiful horse he's ever laid his eyes

50

on about four hundred yards away. Natur'ly
he's got to have the horse, so he sneaks up
like a cat to get a clean shot and send the
rider to his mortal chips without hurtin' the
animal. Then at about twenty yards Bill fires
and drops Tall Bull in a single shot, and
captures the bay like it was all a plan. Now
shortly thereafter, a soldier passes the spot
and marks the distance between Bill's sad-
dlebags and Tall Bull's body at four hundred
yards. And then he makes wind with the
word. Now the point is Bill's like that when
it comes to dealin' with Injuns. He's got
nothin' personal against 'em just so long as
they ain't alive to spoil the truth.

As Buntline's tale unfolds, Sitting Bull, Halsey and
their people are escorted to the Indian Village by Ed
Goodman, Johnny Baker and Osborne Dart. We
watch as Ed points out Sitting Bull's teepee, which is
beside the other teepees. Halsey and Bull have a slight
discussion before Bull makes a broad gesture to the
ridge across the river that overlooks the entire camp.
As the other Indians keep a curious distance from
this famous and celebrated chief, Ed and Johnny
protest with Halsey over Bull's selection. Chief Sitting Bull has indeed arrived.

In the Mayflower, Cody hosts a rowdy macho lunch
affair with McLaughlin, Tompkins, Lieutenant Ford,
as well as his own staff: Salsbury, Burke, Prentiss,
Jules Keen, plus the he-men of the show: Frank
Butler and Buck Taylor. Sonya serves and dodges
advances.

Stories fly from every seat at the table.

BURKE

There I was, seventeen miles from Standing Rock with a broken buggy. Unarmed, to top it off. Should've seen me, Bill, trekking through Indian country in the dark of night. Came across a small party of Sioux, blood in their eyes. Suffice it to say, it'll take more than bloodshot eyes to scare an old Injun fighter like me.

SALSBURY

Major, the only Injun you ever killed was a tubercular Delaware that you worked to death on your granddaddy's farm.

Meanwhile, Burke has heard his name at the other end of the table.

BURKE

Prentiss, were you boasting about me again?

PRENTISS

(*raising glass*)

Sure. I propose a toast to Arizona John's Greatest Coup . . . or, the Peace Pipe Parley!

Just then Ed, Johnny Baker and Dart enter. Actually, Dart waits outside. Ed goes to Salsbury.

ED

Excuse me, Mr. Salsbury, but we got problems.

SALSBURY

What kind of problems, Ed?

ED

Sitting Bull don't want to live with the other Injuns.

CODY

What did you say!

ED

Uh, well, me and Johnny and Dart were showing ...

SALSBURY
(to Cody)
Sitting Bull doesn't like our recommodations.

CODY

What's wrong with 'em?

ED

He didn't exactly say, Uncle Will.

MCLAUGHLIN
(mumbling to himself)
Problems already.

JOHNNY

He wants to live across the river on that flat ridge.

CODY

He wants to live across the river?

SALSBURY

Nobody can cross that river!

MCLAUGHLIN

Big mistake. Beginning of the end.

BURKE

You can't get there from here. No. No.

SALSBURY

Gentlemen, that river has already claimed the lives of six horses, three Blackfoot braves and a bargeload of show equipment valued at sixteen thousand dollars.

JULES

Sixteen thousand three hundred and twenty-nine...

BURKE

Nate proved his dedication on that turn by hocking his Montana ranch. Bailed us out.

FORD

What if somehow he gets over there? Then he'll be in a strategic position to escape.

BURKE

Then he'll be in a strategic position to drown!

MCLAUGHLIN

Cody, the smartest thing you could do is to lock them dog-eaters in the stockade.

Cody is coming back from the bar.

CODY

That's good thinkin', McLaughlin. If we lock all them Injuns in the stockade, then I'd have to storm the damn thing every time I want 'em to perform.

BURKE

I think we have to defer to Nate in this. If Bull and his cronies wish to enter the stockade, they'll have to pay a nickel a head like everybody else. See, that is all that remains of Fort Ruth, the proudest Fort in the West, and it now houses the enterprising Buffalo Bill Museum.

FORD

Cheyenne and Tall Bull, 1871.

MCLAUGHLIN

The Cheyenne burned down Fort Ruth because the U.S. Ninth were all out lopin' their mules.

FORD

That's not true. You were there, weren't you, Mr. Cody?

BURKE

He was not only there but there he was!

TOMPKINS

The way I heard it, some scout killed Tall Bull in that battle, right?

CODY

I certainly did.

FORD

You killed Tall Bull?

55

CODY

(to Burke)

They don't teach history worth a crap in school nowadays.

FORD

How did it happen, sir?

CODY

Well, it's a mighty long story and I'm a touch rusty with it . . .

BURKE & PRENTISS & BUTLER

C'mon, Bill . . . we'd love to hear it.

Cody is already standing.

CODY

Well, us troopers were outnumbered four, five . . . ten to one. We sent out a small scouting party to create a diversion while reinforcements were on their way, but Tall Bull wiped them out in no time. Finally, every last man had retreated to the fort for a last-ditch stand. But I snuck out to see if I could find Tall Bull and maybe end the battle before it began. I made my way to this ridge where I swear I saw half the Cheyenne nation ready to charge. Then I spot Tall Bull aboard this large bay that he'd taken from a farmer name of . . . Baxter after he'd slaughtered the family with the exception of a old woman that he . . . you know.

FORD

Aw. He didn't?

CODY

(*solemn*)

He did. Well, a man ain't a fool unless he knows it. So I ride straight for him, hard as I can. Arrows snap around me but I keep goin'. Then my horse is hit, and as I'm fallin' I catch an arrow in midair and use it as a . . .

BURKE

Flyswatter.

CODY

Yea, a flyswatter, knockin' away everything they send in my direction. Just then Tall Bull decides to make a pass at me himself. Well, I'm waitin' . . . and I'm waitin' until he's at . . . Lord knows how far . . . What would you say, Nate?

BURKE

Thirty yards!

CODY

Thirty yards or more! Then I hurl that arrow with all my strength and catch that big Cheyenne right square in the heart! Naturally his death depressed the remainin' Injuns . . .

Prentiss is already writing the novel in his head.

PRENTISS

Buffalo Bill's closest call . . . or the Fort Ruth Redskins!

CODY

Use 'em both, son.

Say, Bill, I heard another version of how
Tall Bull was killed. And in that one you
killed him with a single bullet at four hundred yards.

CODY

That one ... don't come close to *that* one!

SALSBURY

Gentlemen, I don't think it dispropriate to
play a personal chord here. We all know
sociable chaff is cheap, but history, I mean
real history, is hard-come. And the man I am
about to celebrate is not a mere personation of
a patriot but the true monarch of genuity.
Scout, showman, family person ...

McLaughlin has ceased eating. He stands to look out
the front door at the distant bluff across the river.

SALSBURY

... valued partner. I give you America's National Entertainer, William F. "Bill" Cody.

MCLAUGHLIN

Impossible to cross, huh?

Everyone stretches to see what McLaughlin is looking at. Bull's teepees are rising on the bluff. The men
are astonished, until Cody reassures them with his
nonchalance.

CODY

Boys, on that bluff is *exactly* where I want
him. Then I can keep my eye on him, real
easy, from this chair, here.

58

The others return to their chairs.

> CODY
>
> See, McLaughlin, I'm smart enough to know the difference between a white man and an Injun in a situation like this . . . Injuns always turn down your first offer.

Later that afternoon, Cody, Salsbury, Burke, Prentiss, Keen and Ed lounge on the front porch of the Mayflower as McLaughlin's column of riders fades in the distance.

Margaret's love call is heard from inside the Mayflower.

Salsbury rises and signals to the others that it is time to go. All take the cue and rise. Burke, Prentiss and Keen bid Cody good evening and head down the street toward the Buffalo Bar.

> SALSBURY
>
> Come on, Ed. We have work to do.

Ed hesitates close to Cody.

> ED
>
> Uncle Will? How did Sittin' Bull cross the river?

Cody is a wise man to his nephew.

> CODY
>
> He went from one side to the other. Run along, son.

> ED
>
> Yessir.

SALSBURY

SALSBURY

Ed, come on. We've got work to do. Do you
have the scenarium?

ED

Yessir. Good night, Uncle Will.

Cody disappears inside the Mayflower.

About this time, Sitting Bull and Halsey are seen
leaving Annie Oakley's tent and heading for the
Mayflower, Bull's five braves behind him. Burke,
Prentiss and Keen make a quick about-face back
toward the Mayflower. Salsbury and Ed see the Indians and Cody's entire staff rush into the Mayflower
to warn Cody of the Indians' advance.

Cody is standing in a corner, looking out the window
to the Main Street. Salsbury and the rest rush
through the front door, into Cody's office, shouting
for him. They do not notice that they have rushed
right past the man. Sonya, Cody's housekeeper, is
dusting.

SALSBURY

I'll handle this with Bill. Bill, Sitting Bull's
headed this way. He's got his whole gang.

ED

Uncle Will, they crossed the river again and
they ain't even wet.

BURKE

Our unpredictable friends seem to be on the
warpath and they're headed in this direction.

60

CODY

    I see 'em.

Cody's voice brings the others out from his office again.

BURKE

    They were in Annie's tent.

CODY

    They were?

BURKE

    We're with you, Bill.

Margaret's singing can be heard from the bedroom.

CODY

    Margaret, you can stop singing. We've lost the moment.

Bull and Halsey enter.

MARGARET'S VOICE

    Are you getting sharp with me, Bill?

CODY

    I've got business.

MARGARET'S VOICE

    Well, if you want to apologize, I'll be in your room.

CODY

    Sonya, you can finish that later.

Sonya leaves.

61

A twilight raid, eh, Chief? What's on your
mind?

Sitting Bull has said that he is here by the
will of the Great Spirits and by their will he
is chief.

His heart is red and sweet, for whatever he
passes near tries to touch him with its tongue,
and the bears taste the honey and the green
leaves lick the sky. If the Great Spirits have
chosen anyone to be leader of their land, know
that it is Sitting Bull.

Cody looks at Salsbury.

Halsey, you tell the chief Buffalo Bill says his
green leaves can turn wherever they want . . .
just so long as they know which way the
wind's blowing.
  (*sits; to his staff*)
I think I gave 'em the same murky logic they
use on us.

Undeniable.

Halsey, what Buffalo Bill means to say is Sitting Bull is here to relive great moments in
his history for the pleasure of thousands of
paying customers.

SALSBURY

Buffalo Bill doesn't need an interpreter, Burke!

HALSEY

Sitting Bull says that history is nothing more than disrespect for the dead.

CODY

When did he say that? Doesn't even look like he's interested.

The great chief stands and stares at a stuffed buffalo head on the Mayflower wall.

HALSEY

Sitting Bull's mind is rested and clear and he is ready to negotiate.

SALSBURY

What are you talking about? That's been done. Right, Burke?

BURKE

What? Oh, sure. That's been done and Buffalo Bill has been most generous.

HALSEY

Sitting Bull is ready to negotiate for his people.

CODY

His people?

HALSEY

Sitting Bull wants blankets.

63

CODY

(*sympathetic*)

Oh, they're cold. Nate, do you think we could throw in eight . . . twelve blankets into the deal?

SALSBURY

Eight. Halsey, you've got your blankets.

HALSEY

Sitting Bull wants blankets for all of his people at Grand River.

CODY

Now hold on here. What do you think we are, army surplus?

HALSEY

There are only one hundred six Hunkpapa Sioux left at Grand River.

CODY

(*low*)

My God, Burke, why, five years ago, we counted ten thousand braves alone.

There is a quiet pause.

SALSBURY

Mr. Halsey, the Wild West is proud to give, as a gift, blankets for all of those people. Burke, I want feature cover copy on this!

BURKE

Right. I can use that. We'll splash it over the front pages. The benevolence of Buffalo Bill. Good human-interest stuff. I'll get right on it.

Burke heads for the door. He passes Sitting Bull on the way out. Bull seems not to see him or anyone else.

BURKE

A fantastic follow-up to today's events, Chief. Weary, weary but there's no rest for the press.

But Bull does spot something of interest. It is a giant Music Box. He goes to inspect it. Ed Goodman takes Burke's vacant chair.

CODY

(*to Ed*)
Watch him and make sure he don't steal nothin'.
(*to Halsey*)
All right, that's taken care of. Now we got the Custer act to talk about.

HALSEY

Sitting Bull wants six weeks' salary to send to his people *now*.

CODY

He wants what? Goddamn it, Burke! Where the hell'd Burke get off to? Didn't he take care of any of this?!

SALSBURY

(*calm*)
Halsey, those demands are not only dispropri-ate but completely out of the question.

CODY

Halsey. Tell the chief to sit down. I want to look into his eyes while we talk money.

HALSEY

Sitting Bull knows the value of money but he never talks about it.

CODY

What the hell's that supposed to mean? Ed, that last one wasn't deep enough.

Cody goes to the bar and pours a drink.

SALSBURY

Halsey, what you're asking for is prepayment and we don't do that without a contract.

HALSEY

Sitting Bull will accept four weeks if six is too much for you. Also Sitting Bull will own his own photographs.

CODY

Like hell he will. I own all photographic rights and historics.

HALSEY

Sitting Bull says a man may never let go of his face so he will own his own photographs.

CODY

My ass.

Cody roars to Salsbury while Margaret begins to vocalize in the bedroom.

CODY

Nate. I'm not gonna put up with it. Don't you put up with it. We're not gonna put up with it. Christ, it's bedlam in here.

He storms into his office.

> SALSBURY
>
> Now you see? You've upset Buffalo Bill. So let's put this in the proper respective. Halsey, tell the chief that he's just a part of our show. We pay for work performed. However, if he wants to put his signagraph on a six-month contract that's another matter.

Meanwhile, Ed approaches Sitting Bull at the Music Box.

> ED
>
> How! Me Uncle Will's nephew. Pohaska, me, relatives.

Sitting Bull ignores him in favor of the Music Box.

> ED
>
> Music box. Makes music.

Ed sings:

> ED
>
> "Oh come let us adore him. Oh come let us adore ..."

With no reaction from Bull, Ed tries an Indian chant.

> ED
>
> Eah yea yea, eah yea yea, eah yea yea ...

With still no response, Ed pulls a coin from his coin purse and shows it to Bull before slipping the coin in the machine and turning the handle to start the music.

Wampum.

The machine clicks and finally a gentle song is heard.
Bull takes a glance at the thing and walks away, his
interest flagged. Ed looks disappointed. He tries to
stop the machine. He bangs on it with his fist.

SALSBURY

Ed. Allow that!

From his office, Cody eavesdrops through the leather
curtain. Margaret enters the room and attempts to
lure him to the bedroom. Cody gestures that he'll be
with her presently. She glides back to the bedroom,
humming softly. He continues to listen.

HALSEY

No contract.

SALSBURY

Why not? All of my other top acts have them.

HALSEY

No contract. Sitting Bull will not make a contract that he may not be able to honor.

SALSBURY

Why couldn't he honor it?

HALSEY

Sitting Bull stays only until he sees the Great
Father.

SALSBURY

The Great Father? You mean President
Cleveland.

HALSEY

Yes.

SALSBURY

(*can't resist a laugh*)
Did Burke promise you that?

HALSEY

Sitting Bull no longer accepts promises from white men. His dreams told him this is the place he meets the Great Father. That is why he is here.

SALSBURY

Bull agreed to join our show because he dreamed he would meet the Great Father here?

HALSEY

Yes.

SALSBURY

Isn't he interested in Buffalo Bill and the Show Business?

HALSEY

Sitting Bull wants four weeks' salary and he will send it to his people at Grand River.

SALSBURY

Six weeks, four weeks, it's still prevancement and we refuse to pay.

HALSEY

It is what Sitting Bull wants, not what he demands. If you refuse, his people will only suffer more, again.

Sitting Bull has already stepped through the door, to join his braves. Halsey follows. Cody reappears from his office.

> CODY

Nate, I think we got 'em.

> SALSBURY
> (*fifty percent convinced*)

I know we do, Bill.

> CODY

That Burke is one smart son of a bitch. President Cleveland. Where'd he dream that one up? He's pulled a two-headed rabbit out of his . . .

> SALSBURY

Hat.

> ED

Uncle Will, you're sure smart with Injuns. You pretend to be upset when you're really winnin'.

> CODY

Son, the difference between a white man and an Injun in a situation like this is that an Injun don't know the difference between a question and an answer. That's why they ain't ever sure when they get what they ask for.

Later that night in the dispensary, there is a line-up of cowboys and performers along the bar. Among them are Burke, Prentiss, Jules Keen and, at the far end of the bar, Ned Buntline.

BURKE

Never put off till tomorrow the drinking you can do today.

PRENTISS

(*saluting*)

Drink should never be given to the man who is given to drink.

KEEN

Hooray.

BUNTLINE

(*toasting*)

To Major Arizona John Burke, who's never been a major and never been to Arizona.

BURKE

(*caustic*)

Ned, you're a dear fellow. It's a pity we've turned the page you were written on.

BUNTLINE

You've got it all wrong, Burke. I'm just visiting a gold mine I used to own.

PRENTISS

And the gold has turned to more precious stuff.

BURKE

My Billy is a delightful fellow, and I'd rather be made merry by a fool than be made sad by experience.

PRENTISS

To your tongue, sir.

The Major's tongue is further from his brain than you suppose, Shakespeare.

BURKE

All this tongue has to do, Ned, is to wag in Bison Bill's direction and he'll be over here in no time to toss you out.

BUNTLINE

I'm not so sure. If Bill Cody came over here for anything, he'd end up having a good time. But he can't afford that no more, not with Nervous Nate runnin' things. Profit is all that counts, creative thinking is gone forever.

PRENTISS

To creative thinking!

BURKE

Wrong again, Ned. Why, just moments ago Bill came to my office to congratulate me for promising Sitting Bull he'd meet Grover Cleveland here. He knew a shrewd move when he heard one.

BUNTLINE

Well, I can't imagine you being smart enough to think of that, but you can bet your life that the President will find his way here, someday. Bill attracts Presidents and royalty. Did I ever tell you about Bill and the Grand Duke Alexis of Russia?

BURKE

Not tonight, huh, Ned.

Tonight's the perfect night. Bill's fame as a buffalo hunter spreads after he's supplied the railroad with all the buff meat they'd ever need. He continues to slaughter the brute creatures just to keep the stories alive. Now when the Duke comes over from Russia to hunt, naturally Bill is first in line to snatch the job of scout, knowin' it'll add to his fame.

Now the thing you gotta remember here is that Bill's dying inside to be a hero for all the eastern behaved, and the Grand Duke is his first-class ticket to New York City. Meanwhile, out west, Spotted Tail and his Sioux are hunting buff on the exact spot where Bill plans to take the Grand Duke. Bill, who's always thinking, figures he'll spice up the action with a little shenanigans. Nothin' serious, mind you, just a few warriors riding on the ridgeline doing a catchy war dance or something perilous so Bill can look hot when he clears 'em out. Sure enough, after the group is riding back to the fort, Spotted Tail's bucks appear on the ridgeline as planned. Well, the Duke has an ague fit, but Bill comes to the cure by scarin' the heathens off. Matter of fact, he scares 'em smack into the second cavalry patrol who take it for a real shoot and drop six braves before Bill can explain it was all an act. Now when this breeze blows east, Bill is the shiniest new rank at such mummery as masked balls and opry plays, becomin' once and for all America's favorite hero.

Rehearsal is not the best word for what takes place in the arena between show dates. For if Buffalo Bill happens to be practicing one of his many skills, it is entertainment. At this very moment, the great man is shattering glass-ball targets with two unerring pistols, as Prentiss tosses the balls in the air.

There are two separate groups of Cody lovers and tourists in the arena. The local Buffalo Bill fan club is guided by Jules Keen, while Burke leads Madame Lucille Du Charmes and group on their second visit to the camp.

In addition to Cody, Annie and Frank are practicing their act while Buck Taylor tries to make a gray horse dance upon a gunshot cue. Seated in bleacher seats, observing all of the above, are Sitting Bull, Halsey and the five braves. Sitting Bull is particularly fascinated with Buck Taylor's dancing gray horse.

Burke leads his tour close to Cody. Cody spots the opera singer immediately. He smiles.

BURKE
(at his flatulant best)
Buffalo Bill, allow me to introduce this compelling cadenza in the cornucopia of classicism. This charismatically curvacious canary is a combination of champagne and columbine, the colorful coloratura from Colorado . . . words fail me . . . Madame Du Charmes.

LUCILLE
(correcting him)
Du Charmés.

DWIGHT

Mademoiselle is so delighted with your circus that whenever we are in the area I cannot keep her away.

CODY

Right. Handel's ...

LUCILLE

Renaldo.

She sings, and as she finishes Cody picks up both pistols.

CODY

Double heave!

He breaks two balls simultaneously.

LUCILLE

My, what a shot you are. My second husband, Count Eggenweiler, was a champion trap shooter.

CODY

Trap shootin's a different art, ma'am. Not taking anything away from your ... second husband ...

LUCILLE

Deceased ...

CODY

... but in trap shooting you use a shotgun that sprays. The pistol is a more exacting art. Burke, why don't you take the lady to my personal viewing chair. Nate!

Nate appears.

> **CODY**
> What the hell's going on out there? I wanna show Sitting Bull the act.

> **SALSBURY**
> They're just waiting for the downstick. Here's your scenarium. About Cleveland. At the first, he's marrying a society deb at the end of the month. At the second he's got a Republican Congress to contend with. I think we can safably give Bull the money he wants. If he's waiting for Cleveland to show up, we'll have him for life.

> **CODY**
> All right, but make sure we give him less than he asked for. You see the difference between Injuns and whites in a situation like this is that Injuns gotta be short changed so they can feel cheated. Now go get Bull and Halsey and bring 'em over here.

Bill moves to walk away.

> **SALSBURY**
> Bill.

Salsbury reaches up and tucks Cody's hair under his wig. Cody walks to the viewing stand as Salsbury walks to Bull and Halsey.

Salsbury calls to the Director of the Cowboy Band.

> **SALSBURY**
> Keep the tempos up, Bill.

He also passes Buck Taylor and Isabel with the large gray show horse.

> SALSBURY
> Is the gray doing all right?

> BUCK
> We'll get him to dance or we'll use him for bear bait.

Salsbury reaches the Indians.

> SALSBURY
> Good morning, Chief. Boys. You feelin' better today? I guess we're all feeling better today. Well, Mr. Halsey, if you and the Chief just follow me. Buck, you and Isabel take the gray horse to the other side of the arena.

They follow Salsbury.

> SALSBURY
> Chief Bull, Buffalo Bill has been generous enough to give you a gift of two weeks prevancement as a token of his friendship.

> HALSEY
> Sitting Bull admires the gray horse.

> SALSBURY
> I'd think he'd show more responment to the prevance.

> HALSEY
> Sitting Bull has accepted your money.

SALSBURY

He could at least say thanks.

HALSEY

Sitting Bull will never insult the giver of a gift by acknowledging it.

SALSBURY

You know, Chief, we're the first people to ever show the red and the white without taking sides.

CODY

Howdy, Chief. How're your leaves turnin'?

No response.

CODY

All right, let's get on with it.

SALSBURY

Downstick!

The band starts. Burke steps forward with the scenarium.

BURKE

Ladies and gentlemen, what you are about to see is an absolutely original and heroic scene of inimitable lustre, containing all the genuine material of its kind.

CODY

Don't hog the act, Burke, Ed!

Ed takes the scenarium from Burke. He comes forward to hold it so Cody can read the copy.

CODY

I see General George Armstrong Custer lead-
ing the courageous men of the Seventh Cavalry deep . . . deep . . . deeper into the Injun
territory known as Little Big Horn on a mis-
sion of peace.

PRENTISS

Excuse me, Bill. You know it wasn't really
Little Big Horn. It was the Greasy Grass
River.

CODY

Prentiss, I already got the programs printed.

Several cowboys dressed as Seventh Cavalrymen
trudge into the arena. They are led by Little Johnny
Baker in buckskins and a preposterous golden wig.

SALSBURY

That's Johnny Baker, one of my staff, playing
Custer, making his acting debut.

CODY

"The general halts his troops and they set up
camp, exhausted from their historic and hu-
mane journey carrying the wounds of a cowardly Sioux ambush from the day before."

PRENTISS

Bill, it was a Sioux defense against a cavalry
ambush.

CODY

"As the day ends, the valley is quiet as a
tomb. Then, suddenly, Injuns appear. More
Injuns than anybody's ever seen."

Salsbury begins shouting through his megaphone, cueing the action, prompting the actors.

> SALSBURY
>
> Hurry up. Send the Indians in here.

> CODY
>
> ". . . led by the fiercest and most bloodthirsty Injun of 'em all . . . Chief Sitting Bull."

The Indians enter, led by Dart in full Sioux warbonnet and buckskins.

> CODY
>
> (aside)
>
> That colored's just standing place for you now, Chief. He's the closest thing on my staff to an Injun.

> SALSBURY
>
> Come on, Dart. Act ferocious.

> CODY
>
> "The Injuns sneak past Custer's camp without making a sound . . . which is a sly Injun custom . . ."

> SALSBURY
>
> Sneak, you Indians!

> CODY
>
> "Custer knows it's gonna be a fight for his life, so he writes a quick farewell note to his beautiful wife while the cannon's being loaded."

Johnny Baker stands on a fake rock and writes in a big leatherbound notebook.

PRENTISS

Bill, Custer didn't have a cannon at Greasy Grass River.

CODY

Prentiss, there's reason to believe he had one on order. So, we've just delivered it early.

PRENTISS

I'm just pointin' out the truth of history lessons, Bill.

CODY

It's about time history took a lesson from us! "The Injuns line up across the valley. They outnumber the gallant soldiers of the Seventh by seventy or a hundred to one. The cannoneer, who's only fourteen, fires the cannon . . . in self defense. The Injuns charge."

SALSBURY

Come on. Fire the cannon!

CODY

"There's gunshots, cannon blasts and Injun weapons which are the most deadly of all. Custer's boys drop like flies, but each one dies like a true champion."

SALSBURY

Keep your heads down when you die, out there.

CODY

"The color guard goes down from a bullet in the head, but Custer grabs the flag before it hits the ground at the risk of his own life, 'cause Americans know what's really valuable. Sitting Bull takes advantage of the situation and charges George."

PRENTISS

Bill, the Indians would be shouting, "hoka hey," which is a Sioux war cry meaning "it's a good day to die."

CODY

Good Idea. We'll have Custer's boys shout it. "Sitting Bull uses an old Injun ploy. He fakes Custer into thinking it's gonna be an honorable duel to the death between two great leaders..."

SALSBURY

Come on Dart. Stalk him. Stalk him.

CODY

". . . when Wham! George gets shot in the back by all the other redskins..."

Custer falls. The American flag drops from his hand.

CODY

"Then the bloodthirsty Sitting Bull leaps off his horse and rushes to Custer. The chief lifts the sharpened knife blade in the air and, with the swift movement of a glutton..."

PRENTISS

Guillotine, Bill.

CODY

". . . guillotine, he makes a clean cut of Custer's prize scalp, then treats our country's flag with Injun disrespect."

Dart dances around waving Johnny Baker's wig and stamping on the flag. Dart is not enjoying his part. He mutters.

DART

Wonder why white folks are always makin' fun of what's important to other folks . . .

PRENTISS

Bill, everybody knows that Custer wasn't scalped.

CODY

Prentiss, if I want Custer to be scalped, he'll be scalped. "The End!"

LUCILLE

Mr. Bill. That was without question the most exciting event I've ever seen.

CODY

Well, that's the kinda business we're in.

ED
(to Salsbury)
That was the most exciting thing I've seen. I had goosebumps.

SALSBURY

We're in the goosebump business, Ed.

CODY

Halsey, course I've gotta arrive at the end and chase the Injuns away, but that's only 'cause we call it Buffalo Bill's Wild West. I think we've presented a great tribute to a great chief and highlighted it with just the right amount of dramatics to make both sides look good.

HALSEY

Sitting Bull says the battle did not happen that way.

CODY

Well, we have to overlook things like weather, and geography . . .

SALSBURY

And Dart.

CODY

But you gotta admit it's the chance of a life-time to start a show-business career in such splendor.

Sitting Bull has wandered over to the small table where Cody's guns are placed. He is admiring the beautiful firearms.

HALSEY

Sitting Bull was not present on the battlefield. He was making medicine and dreaming. Sitting Bull will allow you to show his dream. He saw many horses upside down and blue skeletons floating to the promised land.

Halsey, I hope you didn't say what I think you said. Why, I could name fifty chiefs who'd give their eyeteeth just to *ride* in this act.

HALSEY

Sitting Bull will not interfere.

CODY

Interfere? He's gonna do this act, 'cause that's what I choose for him to do!!!

Cody embarrasses himself with the outburst. He turns to Lucille.

CODY

He's just a little stage scared, comin' in as the featured act, right off. He'll be all right. Nate! Talk to 'im.

SALSBURY

Halsey, we're not enemies. We're just artists and entertainers. We're inviting you to join our family. Don't turn us down.

Just then a gunshot goes off, startling everyone. Sitting Bull has picked up one of Cody's pistols that he used to burst the glass balls. The shot has blown a pattern of holes in the side of a prop teepee. It is clear that Cody's pistols are loaded not with single bullets, but buckshot! Bull smiles.

CODY

What's he firing that gun for?

CODY

Hey, put that gun down.

Sitting Bull thinks you are a great marksman.
He can see how you killed so many of his
buffalo!

The black cowboys who are not allowed in the front
of the bar cluster at a window to the front room and
listen to Buntline's stories. As Buntline talks, Frank
Butler sneaks in the back door of the bar and asks
Crutch to fill a medicine bottle with whiskey for him.

Now, a whole lotta folks is sayin' that Bill's
drinkin' has destroyed his memory, but it
ain't true. And he wouldn't let anything do
harm to his regard for history, so you can lay
those stories to rest. But Bill's drinkin', that's
another matter. Why, just two months ago,
Nate Salsbury asks Bill to become a foe of the
cork. And Bill solemnly promises Nate he'll
never be seen under the influence again. All is
rollin' in a straight line until Bill tells Nate
he's given the subject great thought and figures he needs at least one drink a day or
otherwise he'll feel the pain of the saddle
and'll move a lot slower, which means it'll
take Nate longer to earn the same money.
Well, Nate gives in, so long as Bill agrees to
sign a contract to that effect. One drink a day,
no more! And Bill signs. 'Course, Bill's daily
ration is in a schooner the size of a small ship-
ping vessel. But don't get me wrong, Bill
never drinks on the job. No, sir. He's got too
much at stake in the arena, with thousands of
people watchin' every move he makes. It's
that history business again. In Buffalo Bill's

Wild West, history is made with each performance. Only each time it comes out a little different. Crutch, give these boys a drink. They're good listeners.

In the Mayflower, Cody stands, brooding at his office window. He walks to his chair, sits and props his feet on the desk. It is nighttime.

CODY

Margaret!

Margaret enters from the bedroom. She kneels on the floor and embraces him.

MARGARET

Yes, dear.

CODY

Margaret, I've been thinking ... about us.

MARGARET

I'm glad, Bill.

CODY

But the more I think about us, the less I think about Sitting Bull, and that ain't good for the Wild West.

MARGARET

I've never interfered with the Wild West, Bill.

CODY

The point is, the little bastard isn't going to make my life easy. Now I can't deal with him and deal with you and expect to be my best at the both. So I think it's time for you to go.

> MARGARET

Oh, no, Bill. We're just getting close.

> CODY

The quicker you go, the quicker you can start missing me.

Margaret rises sadly.

> MARGARET
> (*singing*)
> Alas, my love, you do me wrong to cast me out discourteously . . .

Cody gently pushes her through the bedroom door.

> CODY

Your buggy will be ready for you in the morning.

And then it is morning.

The sun rises first behind Bull's camp, then stares into Cody's office where Cody is asleep on the sofa. Halsey appears behind him and reaches down to wake him. Cody pats Halsey's hand, assuming it is Margaret's. He doesn't open his eyes.

> CODY

Margaret. I'm sorry. Go back to sleep.

It dawns on Cody then that this is not Margaret's hand. He looks up.

CODY

Halsey! What the hell are you doing here?!

HALSEY

Sitting Bull has come to tell you what he will do in your show.

CODY

Show? My God, the sun ain't hardly up yet.

HALSEY

Sitting Bull's thoughts do not have a time schedule.

Cody tries to cover his head with his night robe, because Halsey has found him with his wig off. He rises and backs out of the room.

CODY

Well . . . go on out there and I'll be with you in a minute.

Salsbury comes out of his bedroom tying the belt of his bathrobe. Ed appears from his room, still in long-handle underwear and an overcoat. Salsbury spots Sitting Bull at the music machine.

ED

What's goin on?

SALSBURY

I don't know. You keep your eye on him. I'll get your uncle.

Ed watches Sitting Bull. Salsbury rushes to Cody's office, is startled to see Halsey standing in the shadows. Cody is at his mirror fixing his wig.

Bill!

CODY

I know. Go find Burke. Halsey caught me with my ... ah!

Salsbury rushes out.

Ed is watching Sitting Bull, who is watching the Music Box. Ed frowns at him and strokes his finger like a schoolboy.

ED

Bad Bull!

Cody's bleary-eyed staff are sprawled around the room. Cody is silently sitting in a chair. Sonya serves coffee. Burke pours himself a drink at the bar. Halsey stands in front of the group. Bull is beside him seated on the steps.

CODY

All right, Halsey. Why don't you tell us why the chief got you up so early.

HALSEY

You will build the village at Killdear Mountain. Sitting Bull's people will be working. Children will be playing. They are waiting for Colonel McLaren and his horse soldiers to talk peace. The Sioux have no weapons and embrace the soldiers with open arms.

As Halsey speaks, Burke and Salsbury huddle. An idea is dawning on Salsbury. Halsey looks more like Sitting Bull than Sitting Bull.

Ladies And Gentlemen!

Presenting

BUFFALO BILL'S

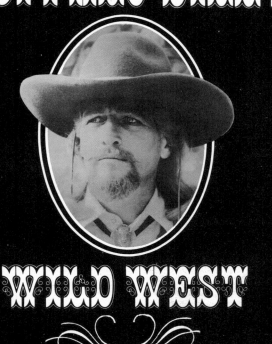

WILD WEST

Paul Newman as Buffalo Bill

Joel Grey as Nate Salsbury

$\mathcal{K}$evin McCarthy as Major John Burke

llan Nicholls as Prentiss Ingraham

oelle Rogers as Lucille DuCharmes

onnie Leaders as Margaret

$\mathcal{H}$arvey Keitel as Ed Goodman

$\mathcal{M}$ike Kaplan as Jules Keen
and John Considine as Frank Butler

Frank Kaquitts as Sitting Bull

Denver Pyle as McLaughlin

ill Sampson as William Halsey with Sitting Bull

$\mathcal{S}$helley Duvall as Frances Folsom
and Pat McCormick as Grover Cleveland

Bufalo Bill's Indian Vill[age]

President Cleveland visits the Indian Village

The Spectators

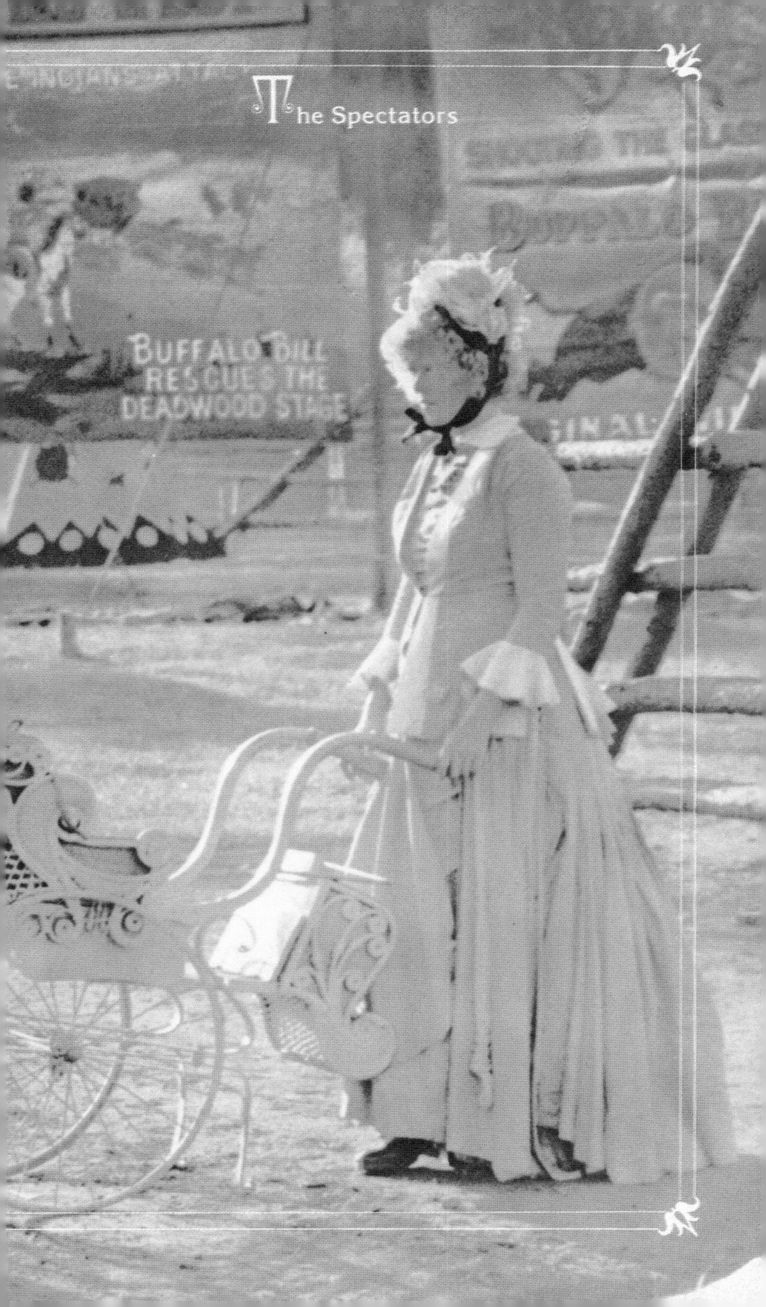

Buffalo Bill's Cowboy Band

The Entertainers

Annie practicing her sure shots

Burt Lancaster as Ned Buntline—the Legend Maker

SALSBURY
Great face and great voice.

BURKE
Great face, great voice, but no act.

Halsey continues without interruption.

HALSEY
Then McLaren's horse soldiers will slaughter
every man, woman, child and dog in the
village. Then Sitting Bull will show how he
sent his people, one hundred men and women,
to Fort Rice to talk treaty with General Sully,
and how during the night Sully killed all who
came there.

BURKE
Bill, obviously these people need talking to.
I got them here with no trouble, and they
trust me. Give me five minutes alone with the
two of them and they'll be eating out of our
hands.

HALSEY
(*continuing uninterrupted*)
Then Sitting Bull will sing . . .

Halsey spreads his arms skyward.

HALSEY
My Father has given me this land.
In protecting it I have had a hard
   time.
The rivers flow with the blood of
   my people.

The winds blow the echoes of lies.
The white man has stolen the truth.
My desire is to love all nature.
My desire is to be loved by all that
    is pure and good.

Salsbury's inspiration is rising.

SALSBURY

If handled properly a singing Indian could be
an act of inspirationment. "Sitting Bull's
Greatest Songs . . ." The New York stage . . .
a full orchestra.

HALSEY

(*continuing*)
Having sung the song of his land, Sitting Bull
will lead five hundred warriors against eight
hundred horse soldiers, and General Sully will
flee from his anger. Sitting Bull will count
many coup.

SALSBURY

Bill, I think I know how to make this scene
work. Buffalo Bill can enter Killdear after
the Indians have attacked McLaren's troops.
We'll concentrate on the action, but I think
the singing's important.

BURKE

Nate, we're not putting on an Indian pageant
here. This is Buffalo Bill's Wild West.

SALSBURY

Burke, please. *I'm* the producer of this show.

Sitting Bull will show how the cowardly white man does not fight unless it is against women or old people or children. That is what Sitting Bull has decided to do.

Halsey has finished and folds his arms. Cody moves from between Salsbury and Burke who continue to bicker.

As he often does in moments of great deliberation, Cody goes to the bar, pours a drink, drinks it, then puts down the cup. He is unnaturally calm. He sits on the step next to Bull.

CODY

Chief, you and me ain't really had a heart to heart yet, but I think it's time. I just heard Halsey talk about five hundred soldiers and dogs and children and God knows what. Now, I gotta figure he's speaking for you or he wants the whole bucket of gold for himself ... Whatever the case, he's got guts. 'Cause he just *insulted* me in my own house. He called me a coward. Says I murdered women and children. And I can't stand for that ... I know you'd feel the same, so it's my decision to see you and him ... Outta here by noon! You got that? You're fired!

Cody storms to his office, mumbling.

CODY

My God, it's harder being a star than an Injun.

The staff is bewildered. Sitting Bull and Halsey walk out of the Mayflower. Salsbury leads a quiet rush to the bar where everyone drinks. Everyone but Ed, who decides to comb his hair.

Because of the early hour, Buntline's only audience in the bar area is Crutch and Rusty, who's having a tooth pulled.

> BUNTLINE
> You know, Crutch, responsibility's a funny thing. And it's different for stars than for ordinary folk.

Buntline takes a bottle that Rusty's been clutching and using for an anesthetic. He pours himself a drink.

> CRUTCH
> Please, Mr. Buntline, this man's in a lot of pain.

> BUNTLINE
> That's why stars spend so much time in front of the mirror, seeing if their good looks and word delivery can overcome their judgment. Just think about it for a second . . .

> CRUTCH
> Not now, Mr. Buntline, please.

> BUNTLINE
> Once a star like Buffalo Bill Cody makes a judgment, it becomes a commitment, and it's gotta stick, no matter what the risk. Yessir! Stars are riskin' a helluva lot more'n ordinary people. Got me, Crutch?

94

The daily wishes of Buffalo Bill Cody are executed in a variety of ways. For instance, at this moment Dart is assisting Margaret into a buggy that will carry her out of the Wild West camp forever. The buggy slowly pulls ahead and Margaret's farewell lament echoes in the distance as Ed Goodman rushes into the Mayflower. He bursts inside Cody's private office where a sober meeting is taking place between Cody, his staff and Frank Butler.

ED

Uncle Will! Uncle Will! Somethin' real bad's goin' on with Annie! She's packin'.

KEEN

He already knows, Eddie.

BURKE

Ed, why don't you go play in the buffalo pen?

ED
(surprisingly tart)
Why don't you? You're dressed for it.

CODY

Oh, God. Is she goin' through with it, Nate?

SALSBURY

Looks that way. I talked to her. So did Burke and Frank. She's not bluffing.

CODY

Is that right, Frank?

BUTLER

Afraid so, Bill. You know I can usually steer her where you want her to go, but not this

time. At first I thought it had somethin' to
do with Buntline . . .

Buntline! Nate, I thought you got rid of him!

You asked me to do it in a certain way. Those
things take time.

Why is everything such a big problem around
here?

Cody arrives at Annie's tent to find that Dart and
Wayne are loading her furniture on a couple of
wagons. Annie is sorting through her clothing, giv-
ing handouts to two young Indian girls who admire
her dresses and things.

I'll only let you test me so far, Missy. Now we
got problems.

Bill, there's no problem.

I could expect disrespect from anybody but
you! Why are you gettin' in the middle of this
anyway? Bull's done nothin' for you.

But he wants to show people the truth. You
can't allow that just once?

CODY

No. I got a better sense of history than that!
Besides, *I* decide what goes in my show, not
some runt Injun and a half-assed half-breed!

She winces.

CODY
(*continuing*)
I'm sorry. Don't you have any whiskey around
this place?

ANNIE

If you send Bull back to Standing Rock, he'll
be killed.

CODY

It ain't my problem. Damn it, Missy, you
won't like it when I find another girl shooting
act.

ANNIE

And you aren't gonna like it when she misses
and misses and misses ...

CODY

Missy, I got ten thousand leaflets printed with
your name on 'em.

ANNIE
(*sarcastic*)
Only ten thousand, Bill?

Cody walks away, talking to himself. He stops in
the street, conversing with an imaginary being of
infinite wisdom. Finally he returns to Annie.

Missy. The little bastard can stay.

(*with a big kiss*)
Thanks, Bill.

Another day and several thousand other dollars later, the roads into the camp are clogged with horses, buggies and wagons bringing spectators to the WILD WEST SHOW.

The streets of the camp are filled with tourists. They inspect the tents and souvenirs and glory. Some pose for photographs with the stuffed bear. Children run about, giggling with excitement. A crowd roams through Buffalo Bill's Indian Village, while another watches Rusty's puppet show depicting the brave exploits of Buffalo Bill.

The Old Soldier stands by the stuffed buffalo on Main Street with a group of little girls. Behind him, there is a long line of people waiting to enter the Buffalo Bill Museum. The pull of the show business is in every visitor's face. And soon each face is riveted toward the center of the arena.

SALSBURY
(*at the podium*)
Ladies and gentleman, I'm Nate Salsbury and on behalf of my partner, Bill Cody, we welcome you to this season's opening show of America's National Entertainment . . . the one and only, genuine and authentic, unique and original, Buffalo Bill's Wild West. Ladies and gentlemen, permit me to introduce our players

... What would the Wild West be without: Brave Cowboys ...

The huge curtains at the head of the arena open and a posse of cowboys race into the arena shooting their pistols. In the backstage area, Halsey leads Sitting Bull's horse next to the fence where Cody's costumes are hung, along with other costumes and props for the show.

> **CODY**
> Halsey, the chief is ready to learn what the show business is all about. And he'll be sorry he didn't do my Custer act, 'cause he's gonna suffer a worse defeat than his. Custer at least got to die. Your chief is gonna be humiliated.

Halsey says nothing in response to this and Sitting Bull sits his little horse, dressed in humble buckskins. He has a single feather in his hair. Around his neck is a string of wooden beads and a simple wooden cross. Cody slips into his gorgeous fringed jacket and puts on his giant beaver hat.

> **SALSBURY**
> (*at the podium*)
> Fierce Indians ...

A band of costumed and painted Indians ride into the arena whooping and hollering. They circle the arena at a clumsy speed. The crowd jeers.

> **SALSBURY**
> Sunburnt amigos from other Americas ... Buck Taylor, King of the Cowboys ... Little Sure Shot, Annie Oakley and Company.

Each act appears as it is announced. The acts range from the naive to the spectacular. The festivities culminate as they always do in BUFFALO BILL'S WILD WEST ... with Buffalo Bill Cody himself. This time he is chasing a well-rehearsed herd of buffalo through the arena on his white stallion, Brigham. And Nate Salsbury commands our attention to introduce the act about which every spectator is more than curious.

SALSBURY

> Ladies and gentlemen, Buffalo Bill's Wild West presents for the first time anywhere the wicked warrior of the western plains, the cold-blooded killer of Custer ... I speak of the untamed savager whose chilling and cowardly deeds created nightmares throughout the West, and made him the most feared, the most murderous, the most colorful redskin alive ... please settle safely in your seats, no fast movements ... You're about to become part of America's history . . . Ladies and gentlemen, I present the battling chief of the Hunkpapa Sioux ... Sitting Bull!

Sitting Bull enters the arena on his small pinto. He rides slowly around the arena, looking neither left nor right. At first the crowd greets this simple spectacle with hatred and laughter.

But Sitting Bull is steady. Finally, the fans erupt with applause as if overwhelmed by the Indian's dignity. Bull exits the arena past Cody, who looks away.

Rusty, Prentiss, Butler, Baker, Keen, etc., are drinking heavily after the first show of the season.

Buck Taylor is passed out on the bar. Buntline's energy is unflagging.

He was truly born to entertain. His calling was to be the Lion of the Show Business long before the show business existed. And if I may dodge modesty, the world owes yours truly a great thanks for recognizing that fact. But I only brought attention to the man. *He* supplied the talent. No ordinary man would have had the foresight to take credit for acts of bravery and heroism that he couldn'ta done. And no ordinary man'd realize what tremendous profit could be had by presentin' the truth as if it was just a pack o' lies with witnesses. And that staff he keeps around could change tomorrow, and nothin'd be any different. Oh, Nate's got more brains than Bill, but he lacks color. And fans don't want their heroes too smart. And Burke, hell, you'll find his name in them press releases more than Bill's. No, Bill Cody can only trust himself and what he picks up with his own senses. And when they fail, he might just see things the way they really are.

The next morning Cody awakens at his desk still dressed from the show. There has been a party in his office; bottles, glasses, cigar butts are strewn everywhere.

Cody looks terrible. There are soft operatic sounds from the bedroom.

Cody slips in the doorway and peeks around the corner. Lucille is at the window singing a lament to

101

her canary. Cody sneaks the atomizer from his vanity table and sprays his mouth. He inhales deeply and steps fully into the room, trying to remember what happened the night before.

> CODY
>
> Good morning. I'm . . . uh . . . sorry 'bout last night, but you know how it is after the season opener . . . The boys like to kick up a little dust and I don't like to let 'em drink alone . . .

He gestures faintly to the bed.

> CODY
>
> I guess I disappointed ya . . . I've become something of a morning man, myself. You know, the whiskey out here isn't very good and . . . You look lovely in the light.

She responds to the compliment. Her face lightens.

> LUCILLE
>
> You haven't said good morning to the Flying Dutchman.

> CODY
>
> Right . . . uh . . . Mornin', bird.

Cody turns his charm on Lucille now.

> CODY
>
> You know, just seeing you standing there with the yellow . . .

Just then gunshots come from the Fort across the street. Buck Taylor and the boys have got Johnny

Baker hung upside down on a rope from the roof of the Fort.

> CODY
>
> What the hell ...

> LUCILLE
>
> They're gonna injure that poor little person. You should do something to help him!

> CODY
>
> Goddamn ... Well, while I'm gone, you just stretch out on the bed and relax. I'll be right back.

Cody rushes outside to see what the commotion is about.

> JOHNNY
>
> Get away from me. Let go. Let go ...

> CODY
>
> All right, boys, stop horsing around. You're not helping my head. Buck, let him down.

> BUCK
>
> Aw, Bill ...

Cody would insist further but he sees something in the distance that stops his speech. On the bluff above the camp, Sitting Bull's teepees are being taken down.

> CODY
>
> Son of a bitch ...

> JOHNNY
>
> What is it, Bill?

Cody rushes to the roof of the Fort for a better look through the telescope. He sees Bull's squaws dissasemble the teepees.

The commotion draws the attention of others now. Salsbury, Keene and Ed appear from the Mayflower.

SALSBURY

    Ed, you better get up there and see if you can help your uncle.

Frank Butler is messing around with Joyce, his favorite laundress, behind one of the tents.

BUTLER

    What's going on over there? You stay here . . .

He runs to join Salsbury and Keen by the fort.

Prentiss and Burke run from the telegraph office into the street.

BURKE

    What's the commotion?

SALSBURY

    (*pointing to bluff*)
Look up there!

BURKE

    Oh, my God!

CODY

    Nate! Burke! Get over here! Goddamn. Sitting Bull's gone. There's nothing but squaws over there. Buck! Get across that river and see what's goin' on!

Ed is looking in the other direction, where he sees Sitting Bull, Halsey and the braves riding away.

ED

Uncle Will . . . the Indians!

Buck Taylor leaps on his horse and races for the river.

CODY

Look at that Buck Taylor ride. He rides like the wind. Look at him go.

Buck dashes into the roaring river. His horse flounders. They are both swept downstream.

CODY

Aw, Buck. How can you do that to me?

ED

Uncle Will . . .

CODY

What is it, son?

ED

Uncle Will. The Indians . . .

He points toward the mountains. Cody swings the telescope around. Ed is standing in the way. Cody sees nothing.

CODY

Why is it so dark in here? . . . Hey, son, get out of the way!

He spots the Indians and roars.

CODY

    Aw! All right, Bull!

Cody rushes down the stairs to join the others.

BURKE

    Buck didn't make it. He's in the river.

CODY

    Somebody cut down Johnny Baker. Boys, I want a posse. A *tough* posse. We ride in ten minutes!

SALSBURY

    Get guns! Provisions!

BURKE

    We're not taking this lying down!

Ed rushes for the Mayflower, slapping his hip and skipping like a kid on an imaginary horse. Cody is already gone in that direction.

Cody enters the bedroom. Angry. Lucille is on the bed, singing.

CODY

    Goddamn it.

LUCILLE

    What's wrong?

CODY

    I got trouble on my hands.

LUCILLE

    That little cowboy wasn't hurt or something?

CODY

No. Injuns. They escaped.

LUCILLE

All of them?

CODY

(*puts on gunbelts*)
No. Just the dangerous ones. I gotta go get 'em.

LUCILLE

How long will you be gone?

CODY

As long as it takes.

He looks at her, disappointed.

CODY

You know I wouldn't let anything come between us and our ...
(*gestures to the bed*)
... except something real like this.

He turns to search in the wardrobe for his jacket.

CODY

Goddamn it, where's my real jacket?

He finds an old buckskin coat.

CODY

Knowing you're waiting here for me will only serve to stiffen my resolve.

He swings his jacket over his shoulders and in the process he knocks the birdcage from its hanger on the wall. The cage crashes to the floor. Lucille leaps from the bed.

> LUCILLE
> You clumsy ... You almost hurt the Flying Dutchman.

> CODY
> I hate birds.

She rushes to the door he has just exited.

> LUCILLE
> Bill Cody, don't you ever harm my Flying Dutchman.

She closes the door and sings a song of revenge.

The men of the WILD WEST camp clog Main Street with their horses and pack animals. The women fill the wooden sidewalks to see them off. Every male but Salsbury and Keen are fitted for traveling. Even Ed has dressed in chaps and big hat. He's on a horse, ready to travel with the rest, when Cody steps onto the porch of the Mayflower to look over his posse.

> CODY
> Ed, what the hell are you doing?

> ED
> Uncle Will, I'm going with ya.

                    CODY
Sorry, Ed, your momma'd never forgive me
if something happened to ya.

                    JOHNNY
Bill, we need every man we can get.

                    CODY
Jules! Take Ed's place. Get on the horse.

                    KEEN
But Bill ...

                    CODY
Get on the horse!

                    ED
Aw, Uncle Will.

He reluctantly gives the horse to Keene.

                    KEEN
I don't ride very well.

A cowboy shoves Keene into the saddle.

                    KEEN
    (timid)
Nice horsy.

                    CODY
    (mounting)
Move out!

The posse races out through the front gate and across
the prairie in the direction of the mountains with

Cody at the lead. Buck Taylor races after them, late from changing his wet clothes. This is what the WILD WEST is all about . . . living legends, living their legends.

In the dispensary, Buntline bends Crutch's ear.

> **BUNTLINE**
> When Bill's dressed for a ride and mounted on that high-steppin' stallion o' his, any doubts concernin' his legends are soon forgot. Yes, Bill's fine physical portrait hides any faults his mind might possess. But even the least seasoned trackers'll tell you, if you don't truly understand what it is you're after, well, you're better off stayin' home.

The sunlit day, that once promised deeds of justice and bravery, succumbs to clouds as a slow-moving posse appears on the horizon, returning to camp.

Ed and Annie watch and wait for the return of the posse. The town's ladies wait behind them. And behind them wait the camp's tamer Indians.

> **ED**
> There they are. Uncle Will! Uncle Will! That'll teach Sittin' Bull a lesson.

> **ANNIE**
> Don't say that.

> **ED**
> It's a question of law and order. Uncle Will's the law and Sittin' Bull is out of order.

110

ANNIE

I don't see Frank.

ED

I don't see Sittin' Bull. I don't see any Indians.
Looks like they killed 'em all.

ANNIE

Don't say that, Ed. Maybe they just didn't find
'em.

ED

Oh, they found 'em.

ANNIE

Maybe they found 'em and they got away
again.

ED

No Injun's ever got away from Uncle Will.

He rushes forward.

ED

I'll open the gate.

From the bar, Crutch watches Cody's posse returning empty-handed. Crutch is shocked at what he
sees . . . or doesn't see.

CRUTCH

I don't see any Injuns with 'em.

Buntline is at his table by the window.

That's 'cause there ain't any Injuns with 'em.

CRUTCH

But Bill's the greatest Injun hunter of 'em all. He led fifteen of the best Injun trackers into a territory he knows like the back of his hand, lookin' for an old man, a giant, and five boys . . . And he came back empty. He ain't ever come back empty. Ever.

BUNTLINE

Yes. Well . . .

Buntline makes a multiple jump on the checkerboard that sits on the table between them.

CRUTCH

Goddamn it, Mr. Buntline. You did it again.

Salsbury is on the roof of the old Fort, waiting the return of the posse. Behind him, Buffalo Bill's Cowboy Band tunes up their instruments.

SALSBURY

I don't see any Indians . . . Sweeney, don't play any music. Turn around so Bill can't see you.

Salsbury hurries to the Mayflower to greet the returning hero. The returning hero and his staff lumber silently into the safety of the Mayflower.

Cody is dejected. He removes his heavy coat and throws it on the big center table. He stares at the oil portrait of himself on his rearing stallion. Sals-

ury and the others enter, equally depressed. They
yally toss their traveling coats on top of Cody's.
urke pours himself and Cody a drink at the bar.

BURKE

We're with you, Bill.

ody ignores his drink. He seems to be apologizing
his heroic image.

SALSBURY

Bill, we made it plain our camp wasn't a
prison.

BURKE

Nat's right. We're not in the prison business.

SALSBURY

(to Burke)
Get to McLaughlin . . . Say that Bull escaped
during the center of the night.

BURKE

Sure, and he tried to burn down the arena
first.

ED

(to Prentiss)
I sure thought you'd catch 'em. They weren't
that far ahead.

PRENTISS

Ed, why don't you go close the gate?

ody puts his hand on Ed's shoulder.

CODY

Ed, have Dart give Brigham a rubdown.

He then disappears into his bedroom. There is silent moment.

BURKE

You know I been with him for eleven year and I've never seen him not even touch hi drink.

SALSBURY

It's my fault. I should have fired that damne Injun.

ED

I don't care what anybody says . . . God bles Buffalo Bill.

There is more silence, then a gunshot from the bed room.

SALSBURY

My God! He shot himself!

They all rush for the bedroom, bullets comin, through the wall and hailing around them.

Salsbury and the others arrive in Cody's bedroom t find Cody firing his gun at Lucille's canary, whicl has escaped from its cage. Lucille is trying her bes to stop Cody.

LUCILLE

If you do any harm to the Flying Dutchmar it'll be the end of you, Bill Cody.

CODY

Button up!

Cody fires and breaks a window, providing an escape route for the bird.

LUCILLE

He's gone. My beloved is gone.

Lucille rushes for Cody. Burke intercepts her.

CODY

I hate birds.

He bulls through the crowd at the door and storms into his office, on his way to his bar.

But Cody is stopped in his tracks when he sees Halsey and Sitting Bull looking in the front door of the Mayflower. Salsbury and the others crash behind Cody.

CODY
(*pulling them out of view*)
Hold it!

SALSBURY

What's wrong?

CODY

Bull and Halsey are out there.

SALSBURY

How could they be?

CODY

They musta tracked us back here. Come here.

The group huddles to consider a course of action.

The Indians wait patiently until Cody strides into
the meeting room and hails the Indians as if they
were all the best of friends.

CODY

Come on in, boys!

Cody flops in his chair. The others stand behind him.

CODY

Couple of the buffs got loose and we were
obligated to chase 'em down . . . Where've you
been?

HALSEY

It is the first moon of the month . . .

SALSBURY

(miffed)
That's not what Buffalo Bill asked you.
Where've you been?

HALSEY

During the first moon of the month, Sitting
Bull visits the sun and the mountains while
his squaws move his teepees to the moon's path.

SALSBURY

Damn it, Halsey. Stop sunning and mooning
us and tell us where you've been.

116

CODY

You tellin' me you've been sitting in the mountains all day?

HALSEY

Yes.

CODY

That was a mite dangerous, don't you think?

HALSEY

Sitting Bull is familiar with the mountains.

CODY

What if I'da sent somebody out after you?

HALSEY

Sitting Bull was not hiding. Sitting Bull has been with the mountains and now he realizes that he must do more in your show than ride the pinto.

BURKE

(*relieved*)

There you have it. We're back in business. Foes in '76. Friends in '85.

SALSBURY

Quiet, Burke. I still don't know what he's talking about.

CODY

Explain what you just said.

HALSEY

Sitting Bull has decided that he will do the only thing that he had seen here that he would want to show his people.

CODY
(*suspicious*)
What's that?

HALSEY

Sitting Bull will make the gray horse dance.

With nothing more to be said, the chief and his interpreter leave the Mayflower. On their bluff beyond the river, Sitting Bull's squaws move teepees into the path of the moon.

It is another day and Cody is locked into a meaningful stare with the mirror while the entire company waits outside for a group photograph of the complete WILD WEST.

CODY

In closin', Halsey . . . ah, too official . . . Halsey, you tell the chief, the *only* way I coulda avoided seein' you Injuns is . . . you were hidin' in a cave! You *never went* to the mountains! Good. But I understand *why* you lied . . . Uh, I understand why . . . uh, *you* gotta look good in front of *your* people . . . just like I do in front of . . . mine. No, that ain't . . . Sure, why not? And, uh . . . and because I'm *generous,* and *flexible* . . . Oh, that's real good, generous *and* flexible . . . Uh, I chose to overlook the entire episode!

He is satisfied with his explanation and smiles.

Outside Lucille has followed Margaret's fate and she sits in a buggy while a black cowboy loads the last of her luggage. The driver pulls away, and Lucille sings a lament as she passes the group photographer where Burke shouts orders to the performers in order to pose them properly. Brewster, the camp photographer, is with his camera and flash pan in front of the group.

Several cowboys are jostling the ladies inside the Deadwood Stage.

> BURKE
>
> Boys, boys, you wranglers on top of the stage-coach. Could you keep still? I'm sure the ladies enjoy a bouncing around now and then, but this isn't the time. We must all be still for the picture. Thank you. Nate, where are you? I can't see you.

> SALSBURY
>
> I'm here, Burke.

Salsbury is sitting on the porch behind several performers and staff.

> BURKE
>
> Will you tell Bill we're ready, please?

> SALSBURY
>
> Are you ready, Bill? He says he's ready.

Cody steps out of the Mayflower and takes the keystone position in the group.

CODY

Ladies and gentlemen and Injuns, I didn't
know you were waiting for me. My apologies.
Go ahead. Fire it.

BURKE

All right, Brewster. We're all set.

Burke gets into position and the picture would be
taken except that a black cowboy, Wayne, runs in
from the direction of the telegrapher's office. He calls
to Dart.

WAYNE

Psst. Dart. Hey, Dart.

BURKE

(*irritated*)
What is it, Wayne? Dart, go see what the
darky wants. And you can thank him for
taking you out of the picture. Brewster, we're
ready.

Brewster would take the picture but Dart and
Wayne's conversation distracts him.

DART

What do you want, Wayne? I'm trying to get
my picture took.

WAYNE

(*breathless*)
There's a telegram comin' in over the wire. It's
from the President of the United States.

DART

Are you kidding me, Wayne?

WAYNE

I just saw it comin' over the wire.

DART

My God.

Dart turns and shouts to the whole company.

DART

There's a telegram coming over the wire from the President of the United States!

With that announcement the entire company rushes forward toward the telegraph office. Cody waits a few seconds and marches down the street behind the rest, whistling his theme song as if such honors were his due. The only members of the troupe left in front of the Mayflower are Halsey and Sitting Bull. Halsey looks into Brewster's camera with pride.

HALSEY

You may take the picture now.

Everyone else gathers around the telegraph office. Cody makes his way through the crowd, reads the telegram, then returns to the Mayflower, triumphantly. Burke reads the telegram aloud.

BURKE

"The President of the United States has chosen to celebrate the first stop of his honeymoon excursion with the former Frances Folsom in Buffalo Bill's Wild West Camp, at Fort Ruth . . ."

The crowd is amazed.

"The scheduled time of arrival is Thursday, October 18, at eight o'clock . . . P.M." *Night!*

SALSBURY

Night! We've never done a night show before.

ED
(*calling after Cody*)
The President of the United States is comin' here, Uncle Will. It's just like in Sitting Bull's dream.

The bar is full of people excited by the news of the President's coming. Buntline has got an audience.

BUNTLINE

Injuns gear their lives to dreams. And once an Injun dreams, no matter how farfetched it is, he'll wait till he dies for it to come true. White men, they're different. They dream 'cause that's the only time things go their way. Buffalo Bill Cody don't dream at all. He likes to think he's a dreamer but he's just a sleeper. Now I bring this dream business up right now 'cause things are startin' to take on an unreal shape. Just think. Sitting Bull arrives in camp 'cause he's dreamed the President's gonna meet him here. The wire comes with the same news. Now Bill can't believe in somebody else's dream 'cause he don't have none of his own, so there's no way he's fully prepared to understand what has taken place. But Sittin' Bull, he never doubted any of it for one minute. Just put yourself in that Injun's position. First you sit in your teepee and you dream.

122

Then you go to wherever your dream might come true, and you wait for real life to catch up. Now, I ain't an expert on the subject, but what Bull does is sure a hell of a lot cheaper than mountin' a Wild West show, which is just dreamin' out loud.

If mounting a WILD WEST SHOW is just dreaming out loud, as Buntline says, then mounting a *night* WILD WEST SHOW comes very close to staying awake.

Anything that will burn has been used to illuminate the arena, and the results are spellbinding. The V.I.P. box is stuffed with the Cleveland entourage: Cleveland, Frances Folsom, O. W. Fizician (the speech writer), Nina Cavalini (the opera singer), General Benjamin and other assorted guests plus Cody's staff: Ed, Burke, Prentiss and Jules.

Salsbury is at the podium. He introduces a special version of the Grand Parade, one that only includes Cody.

SALSBURY

Mr. President, Mrs. Cleveland, honored guests. I'm Nate Salsbury and I can tell you that Nate Salsbury has never been as proud in his long career in the show business as he is tonight to present our first after-dark request performance and to dedicate it to you, our highest American and your fine new wife. And it makes me triply proud tonight to open our show in the big way by introducing one great American to another great American.

Mr. President, Mrs. Cleveland, lustrous guests, meet America's National Entertainer, the man who *is* the Wild West. The honorable William F. Cody, Buffalo Bill.

All eyes turn toward the entrance where a fire hoop has been placed. Upon a musical cue, Cody and Brigham leap through the flames and approach the V.I.P. box, where he addresses the President.

CODY

Mr. President and Mrs. First Lady, and all you other distinguished guests. Welcome to my Wild West. Most people will tell you it's the father of the new show business. And, well, may the sun never rest on this great nation unless it comes up again in the morning. I hope you enjoy our wedding gift to you.

He tips his hat and rides out.

BURKE

Buffalo Bill writes all his own sayings, Mr. President.

Fizician whispers to Cleveland, providing him with a line.

CLEVELAND

All great men do.

Various performers stand near the podium watching the President. Frank and Annie stand side by side.

BUTLER

My God—look at the President, Annie.

Grover Cleveland!

Now there is a star!

I wanna shoot for him tonight, Frank.

I do, too, honey.

Mr. President, Mrs. Cleveland, most welcome guests, here's a shining star in the American show business without peer. A child of a woman who has made it clear all across these United States that this woman's place is in the arena and in America's hearts. Mr. President, Mrs. Cleveland, chosen guests . . . the foremost woman marksman in the world, Miss Annie Oakley, assisted by her husband, Mr. Frank Butler.

Annie and Frank glide across to the center of the arena as the band plays the "Little Miss Sure Shot Serenade." They dance to the music as Annie lifts her guns and Frank tosses glass balls in the air.

The act is a bullet ballet. Frank picks up playing cards, which Annie pierces. On the most difficult shot, she also pierces Frank's shoulder. The act is suddenly over. Annie and Frank quickly dance a retreat from the arena. Frank disguises the wound by tossing his coat over his shoulder. Salsbury begins talking over the tripliphone desperately to cover their unexpected exit.

125

Aren't they skillful? You know it was in
honor of Mrs. Cleveland's interest in the arts
that Annie and Frank has specially choreoed
their act tonight. And you can shake that
lady's peerless hand later tonight in Buffalo
Bill's famous Mayflower at the Grand Reception in your honor.

And so the historic theatrics proceed through all the
usual acts of the WILD WEST culminating in a spectacular version of the Attack on the Settler's Cabin,
wherein Buffalo Bill rescues the captured daughter
from peril by appearing and scaring off the savage
Indians with his heroic image.

Salsbury then introduces Sitting Bull. The entrance
curtains open and the great chief rides in on the
tall gray horse.

All eyes look toward the entrance where the little
old man on the gray mare enters and slowly circles
the arena as if his heart couldn't stand anymore.

FRANCES
Oh, Grove, he's just a little old man.

CLEVELAND
Well, maybe the horse is too large.

Bull travels across and through the unreal light until
he stops in front of the box. Cody watches through a
slit in the podium backdrop.

Bull speaks to Cleveland in Sioux.

CLEVELAND
(looks to Fizician)
I don't understand a word he's saying. Do you?

FIZICIAN
No. But I can guess.

Sitting Bull has finished his speech. Halsey steps outside the backdrop. Cody looks at him and at Bull.

Bull slowly reaches under his buckskins. It appears he has pulled a revolver. He brings it up to Cleveland's face. Frances shrieks.

Cody reaches for his pistol.

But Bull has pointed the pistol skyward and fires. The mare does its dance. The Presidential box begins to grin collectively, then laugh, and finally roars. Cody sighs.

CODY
That damn Injun ain't professional.

The band strikes up a large, syrupy western theme and a certain comic madness prevails in the arena.

Later that night we attend a formal reception for the Presidential party. No one is comfortable. There is a reception line, with Burke and Salsbury directing.

Cleveland is the king of inanity and Frances the queen. Salsbury reflects both the strain and jubilation by drinking too much. Frank Butler is having the worst of it, though. As he goes through the line,

eyery person claps him on his concealed wound. He
manages to get to the punch bowl where little Joyce
is serving.

                    JOYCE
        Frank. I have to talk to you about something.

                    FRANK
            (*whispering*)
        Not here, Joyce.

                    JOYCE
        But I have something to tell you.

                    FRANK
        What is it?

                    JOYCE
        I'm pregnant.

Frank hurries across the room to find a spot of wall
to lean on and downs his drink.

Only now do we spot Cody, and it is obvious why he
has been ignoring the President. He is across the
room, ogling the opera singer.

                    CODY
            (*to Nina*)
        Excuse me. I heard you sing Rossini's "Barber
        of Seville"—it was a triumph.

                    NINA
        Yes, it was a triumph. I always have triumphs
        when I sing. You should have heard me sing

at the Theatra Del Roma. That's in Rome, you know.

She sings a few bars for him. Cody grins.

Frances interrupts them to introduce the opera singer to the party. Nina Cavalini sings, and her luscious voice captivates Cody more than the rest. When Nina finishes, she makes a move in his direction. He takes her hand. Kisses it.

> CODY
> That was lovely.

He lowers his voice to a seductive whisper.

> CODY
> Why don't you make plans to stay here for a few days. I'll show you the *real* Wild West.

> NINA
> I'd love to, William, but my life with General Benjamin is wild enough.

She walks past Cody to General Benjamin, who kisses her hand and leads her away. Cody collects himself and heads for the bar and his private stock. He is shocked and hurt by the rejection.

As Nina and the General walk past the door, Halsey and Bull appear. Nina shrieks. Ed turns to see the Indians. He is furious at the intrusion. Young Ed is maturing.

> ED
> Bull, what are you doing? . . . Halsey, what is he doing here?

HALSEY

Great Father is here in answer to Chief Sitting Bull's dreams.

ED

This party is by invite only, and you don't have an invite. No more Bull! You go. That way.

He points to the back door.

CLEVELAND

Let them enter. I think the chief is a wonderful comedian, Mr. Gordman.

ED

Goodman.

HALSEY

Great Father, Sitting Bull has waited to ask you a very simple thing for his people.

CLEVELAND

He has? . . .

Fizician whispers in the President's ear.

CLEVELAND

Mr. Halsey. I remind you that in government nothing is simple.

HALSEY

This simple request will satisfy Sitting Bull's people for the length of time, Great Father.

Again upon the prompting of Fizician:

CLEVELAND

Let me point out that I'm only "Great Father" four years at a time...

Fizician whispers. The President repeats.

CLEVELAND

And another thing, I'm facing a Republican Congress. No, Mr. Halsey, nothing is simple. I suggest you deal directly with your local agent. He'll be able to help you much better than I.

HALSEY

We have talked to the agents. They will not help.

CLEVELAND

Isn't that a good indication your request is impossible?

HALSEY

But Sitting Bull's request is very simple.

ED

Halsey, the President of the United States is trying to tell you that nothing is simple. Don't you understand American?

HALSEY

Sitting Bull's request is simple. Sitting Bull's dream said that he would meet the Great Father here and Sitting Bull hoped the Great Father would honor his request.

Fizician tries to help Cleveland, but the President is on firm ground now and he ignores the advice.

CLEVELAND

I'm very sorry, sir, but there's nothing I can do about it.

HALSEY

But the Great Father has not heard Sitting Bull's request.

CLEVELAND

That's the point! It doesn't make any difference. It's out of the question.

Bull turns to leave. Halsey burns a moment, then follows. There is a hush as Cody steps over.

CODY

Well, Mr. President, I now see *why* you're President. You're most at ease with the murky frontier style. You see, sir, the difference between Presidents and chiefs in a situation like this is a President knows enough to retaliate before it's his turn.

CLEVELAND

(*to Fizician*)
Why didn't you say that? Remember it. We'll use it for the convention next month.

CODY

Well, everybody, gettin' late and I'm sure the newlyweds are tired.

CLEVELAND

As a matter of fact, we are.
(*squeezes Frances*)
It's been quite an eventful day.

CODY

It's a pleasure to offer you my own personal bed. It's pract'ly new. And, Mrs. Cleveland, I can think of no more beautiful woman than you to be the first to sleep on it.

FRANCES

Oh, Buffalo Billy.

CLEVELAND

Where will you sleep, Buffalo Bill?

ED

You can sleep with me, Uncle Will.

CODY

No, Ed. Mr. President, I've learned it ain't that good for ya to live in comfort all the time. I'll sleep on the prairie, under the stars, listening to the lullaby of the coyotes.

CLEVELAND

It's men like you that have made this country what it is, Buffalo Bill.

Later that night Cody, having given his bed to the President, walks down Main Street, looking for company. He spots Dart coming out of the mercantile tent.

CODY

Work done, Dart?

DART

Yessir, Mr. Cody. Got the place spic and span.

133

CODY

That's fine, boy. Too bad Injuns ain't learned a thing from you coloreds. But, s'pose if they had, there'd be nothin' to fuss about. And Injuns love to fuss.

DART

Mr. Cody, I ain't never thanked you for givin' me the opportunity to work for ya.

CODY

No need to thank me, Dart. It's part of my upbringin' to do what I can for coloreds.

DART

How's that, sir?

CODY

My father, rest his soul, died tryin' to keep slavery out of Kansas.

DART

How'd he do that, sir?

CODY

Dart, who do you have to have to have slavery in Kansas?

DART

You need niggers, sir.

CODY

Right. So instead of lettin' 'em get *into* slavery, he fought to keep 'em all *outta* the state.

DART

Oh.

Cody is feeling magnanimous tonight. Lonely, too.

CODY

C'mon, Dart. I'll buy you a drink. Even let you sit out front with the white men.

DART

No, thanks, Mr. Cody. Gotta feed your horse.

Dart leaves Cody forlorn. He turns to see Annie's tent. Her silhouette is on the canvas walls. He walks to the tent just as Frank's silhouette appears and embraces hers. Cody turns and faces to the bar, where some lights are still shining.

Cody cracks the back door of the bar and peers in. Buntline and Crutch are there. Cody enters and walks to the bar, pretending not to see Buntline.

CODY

Crutch, gimme a bottle of bourbon.

Crutch looks at Cody with surprise. Obviously Cody doesn't appear here often.

CRUTCH

Sure, Mr. Cody.

Cody pours himself a shot.

BUNTLINE

Well, I'll be damned. Buffalo Bill himself.

CODY

(cool)
Hi, Ned.

135

BUNTLINE
Buy an old friend a drink.

CODY
(to Crutch)
Another glass.

BUNTLINE
I was beginnin' to think you didn't exist, Bill.
But here you are in the glorious flesh, and
what a sight for sore eyes.

Buntline steps to the bar, but keeps his distance.

BUNTLINE
Oh, you sure passed me by. Like plantin' a
seed and watchin' it grow to a tree that's too
tall to climb. You got everything you ever
wanted, friend. Even got the President of the
United States sleepin' in your bed right now.

CODY
Forget that stuff, Ned. Let's get drunk.

BUNTLINE
Can't forget it, Bill. Just lookin' at you reminds me of it.

CODY
It's a living.

BUNTLINE
Oh, no, Bill. Way past livin'. Why, a hundred
years from now they'll still be shoutin' your
name. You're not one of the boys no more,

Bill. You're not like ordinary folk. Gives me goosebumps just bein' this close to ya.

CODY

You still got the knack, don't you, Ned?

BUNTLINE

You make it easy, Bill.

CODY

You prob'ly were the best there ever was.

BUNTLINE

Why, thanks, Bill.

CODY

And I'd sure like to have you back in the show, but frankly, Nate can't stand the sight of you. And, Ned, nostalgia ain't what it used to be. But if you hang around maybe I could find something for you to do. Can't promise ... but I'll try.

BUNTLINE

Bill, you throwin' me a crumb to nibble on?

CODY

Aw, Ned, I'm just saying we got a few years invested in each other and that's what friends are for.

BUNTLINE

You ain't changed, Bill.

CODY

I ain't supposed to. That's why people pay to see me.

BUNTLINE

Well, this has been the most sobering experience of my life. Damn near a religious awakening.

He toasts Cody with his drink.

BUNTLINE

Buffalo Bill. It's been the thrill of my life to have invented ya.

The words stun Cody.

BUNTLINE

Crutch, what do I owe ya?

CRUTCH

Nothin', Mr. Buntline. You don't owe me nothin'.

BUNTLINE

Good. 'Cause that's what I got here, nothin'.
(*moves to the door*)
Now I'm off to California to preach against the vultures of Prometheus.

He is gone.

CODY

Ned!

Buntline's horse is tied outside the bar. He pulls his greatcoat from behind the saddle and puts it on.

CODY
(*in the bar doorway*)
Ned!

They stare at each other. Cody shrugs. Buntline lashes his mount and the horse leaps forward. Buntline shouts over his shoulder.

BUNTLINE
See you in hell, Bill!

He races out of the camp and leaps the fence that separates Buffalo Bill's WILD WEST and the outside world. The prairie darkness is so black we never see Ned Buntline land.

A season later, the first light snow of the year has fallen. The WILD WEST is cold and desolate. Smoke rises from the stovepipes of the various tents. A few Indian ladies cross Main Street wrapped in blankets. Frank Butler hurries from a rendezvous back to the warmth of Annie's tent.

The camp is in hibernation.

In the Mayflower, a man named William F. Cody, "Buffalo Bill" to most of us, is balancing himself against imaginary objects. He springs awake from his bed. Something has happened to America's National Entertainer. Something big.

CODY
What! What was . . . I don't dream! I ain't alone—I ain't never—Yes, you are . . . No, I'm not . . . Yes . . . No . . . I been here . . . Who's doin' that wigglin'? . . . Mercy on us . . . Thought I was bittin by that fierce dog of yours, Missus . . . but it musta been a burr . . . been a . . . wiggling! Ladees and . . . ladeees and . . . the one . . . the . . . legendary . . . the . . .

139

Somehow, Sitting Bull is standing silently in the center of the room in full regalia. But it isn't really Sitting Bull. Just a drunken delirium.

CODY

Don't . . . He ain't really around . . .
    (*he sees his hair in the mirror*)
They're all doin' it, Lulu . . . George, Jack, Wild Bill . . .
    (*he sees Bull*)
All right . . . Yes, fine, all right . . . suit yourself . . . You ain't . . . you ain't even the right image!
    (*or does he?*)
Halsey, tell the chief that I think *you* got all the brains . . . Tell him! Damn half-breed, I'll tell him myself . . . Halsey's got all the brains! But Halsey don't mean a word he . . . he says! He don't mean it, and that's how come it sounds so *real!*

Cody strikes his famous pose.

CODY

Real! I was a boy . . . eleven . . . *Nine!* Shot the big buff . . . right smack . . . right square in the . . . *God meant for me to be white!* . . . It ain't easy . . . I got people with . . . *no lives* . . . livin' *through me!* Proud people! People to worry about . . .
    (*there is pain*)
. . . Sister, I'm sorry I cannot help you and furnish you with the . . . You see, I'm short of . . . I'm . . . Let me tell you something . . . My daddy . . . he died on me . . . he died without seein' me as I . . . as a star! . . . Tall, comfort-

140

able . . . profitable . . . good-looking . . . A lesson, Chief . . . *The* lesson, Chief . . . Custer was a good man . . . Gave coffee and sugar to the Injuns . . . Stop it! Custer was a good man. He gave the Injuns a reason to . . . to be famous!

(stoops)

In one hundred years . . . in other people's shows . . . I'm still *Buffalo Bill* . . . star! You're still . . . *The Injun!* . . . Room for only one . . . only the . . . Look at you . . . you wanna stay the same! That's goin' . . . *backwards!* Buntline, damn you . . . *deserter!* I'm curious . . . All my women're curious . . . All my fans're curious . . . And I let 'em *pay* for it! And I give 'em what they *expect!* You can't do . . . you let 'em . . . *laugh!* Ha! They laugh at you! . . . Chief, son . . . the difference 'tween a white man and a Injun in *all* situations is . . . a Injun is red! Simple as that. Otherwise, we're all the same . . . But a Injun is red for a real good reason . . . So we can tell 'em apart!

(the painting)

Ain't he riding this horse all right? If he ain't, then why did all of you mistake him for the king? Chief, I'm gonna make you a gift of that dancin' gray. You two deserve each other. Shoot a gun and you . . . dance. Maybe you *need* each other. Well, I do what I do for *me!* 'Cause when you do that, you're gonna live a little longer. *It makes me true!* 'Cause truth is whatever gets the loudest applause! Run away . . . run away . . . It's *your* problem that the white man don't listen . . . not his! *You're* the one who's gotta suffer . . . White man can just forget the whole . . . damn . . .

thing . . . Old Bunt, catch me . . . catch me . . .
I will not die . . . I will not . . . I ain't got no
one to talk to but . . . you. And you ain't even
. . . here. Carve it . . . Carve your names. All
of you! Carve your names and celebrate the
event!

Time reveals itself to BUFFALO BILL'S WILD WEST
through the executive staff pacesetters, their memory trying to cheat time by reflecting its passing
in their style. Success. Now, the entire staff is
spread about the Mayflower in sober business discussion. Prentiss, looking more like Ned Buntline
every day, reads his latest Buffalo Bill Cody auto-
biography to Burke, who has quieted his appearance
if not vocalness. Ed has grown a mature moustache,
while Jules Keen resembles a rich bank executive.
Nate is mellow, retiring and prosperous.

As for Cody, he never changes. He's not supposed
to. He resembles a great sculptured work of art,
whose eyes shine from without. Presently he is being
made up in his chair while the business of the WILD
WEST that bears his name goes on smoothly without
him.

ED

I'm talking to the people at Kansas Pacific
Railroad. I'm sure I can cut their bid in half.
They want the country to know they service
Buffalo Bill's Wild West.

SALSBURY

Good. You have my go-ahead on that. Jules,
you have anything?

Well, the new raise in prices has more than offset the increase in costs, and this season's run of the show should gross three hundred thousand more than last year.

SALSBURY

Fine. What about the Rhode Island land sale?

ED

I'm working on that.

Salsbury walks around the table now to Cody. The makeup man is painting some of the gray out of Cody's beard.

SALSBURY

Bill, listen to me. For today we're cutting the glass-ball shooting. What they want to see is you ride.

CODY

(*mechanically*)
Sure. Sure. Nate. Say, you was in Europe, wasn't you? Did you give my regards to the Queen?

SALSBURY

Sure, Bill. Everybody asked about you.

Salsbury walks back to the table. Ed moves to Cody.

ED

Bill, this will be our best year ever. We'll gross over two million.

143

CODY

Fine, son. You know I hold the Pony Express record for a continuous ride. Three hundred and twenty-two miles and ...

ED

(*somewhat sympathetic*)
I know.

CODY

Have a drink with me, son. For old times.

ED

Too early for me, Bill ... Ah ... Uncle Will, how're ya feelin'?

CODY

(*hollow*)
I feel great, Ed. I feel great. I could go on forever.

ED

That's great, Bill.

Ed gives him a pat and leaves Cody alone with his makeup man.

CODY

Monty, did I ever tell you I hold the Pony Express record for the longest continuous ride? Three hundred and twenty-two miles and eighteen horses.

Later that day, a record number of fans line the main street of the WILD WEST camp as every member of the show parades toward the arena. Cody is there, offering splendorous satisfaction to those loyal fans who have paid increased rates to witness his greatness.

And, today, all of these people will be shown an act that is completely new and exciting.

From opposite sides of the arena, two horsemen appear. The banners announce, "Buffalo Bill vs. Sitting Bull: A Challenge for the Future." The fans mumble, teased with delight. Sitting Bull is fully dressed with feathers, war paint, jewelry, a proportion that satisfies all preconceptions, mostly because Sitting Bull is played by William Halsey.

Johnny Baker announces.

JOHNNY
Ladees and gentlemen, for the first time in the history of the show business, we present a conflict between two of the greatest warriors western civilization has ever known. With spectacular realism, Buffalo Bill, known as "Pahaska" to his native adversaries, has been challenged by Chief Sitting Bull, the bloodthirsty savage leader of the Hunkpapa Sioux, to a duel to the death. Buffalo Bill has accepted for his beloved country. *It is his moral obligation!*

As Cody and Halsey stalk each other in the arena, Cody's staff watches the action from the press area near the podium.

145

Frank Butler stands off to one side, talking with Joyce. She is now clearly in the late stages of her pregnancy.

> **BUTLER**
> Well, I sure am glad that everything is going well for you. You're lookin' fine. You do know that I'd love to be of some help, but you understand my position.

> **JOYCE**
> If it's a boy I'm gonna name him after you.

> **BUTLER**
> Oh, dear, I'm very honored by that, but I don't think it would be good judgment. People might get the wrong idea. Don't you understand.

> **JOYCE**
> Well, maybe you'll be leaving Annie.

> **BUTLER**
> Don't talk like that.

Prentiss Ingraham has come running into the arena, breathless, waving a telegram. He runs past Butler toward Jules Keen and Annie who are talking in the press area.

> **BUTLER**
> What's going on?

Butler follows Prentiss.

> **PRENTISS**
> They've shot Sitting Bull.

He shows Keen, Annie and Frank the telegram
Annie's face freezes in horror.

BUTLER

I'll be damned.

KEEN

Oh, my God!

Annie begins to weep openly.

BUTLER

It's all right, honey. Don't cry.

BURKE

What is it? What's wrong?

SALSBURY

What's the matter, Annie?

KEEN

Sitting Bull's dead.

SALSBURY

What?

ED
(*calmly*)
She means Halsey. She's upset that Halsey's
playing Sitting Bull.

BUTLER

No. It's the *real* Sitting Bull.

PRENTISS

McLaughlin's police at Standing Rock. They
say he was trying to escape. He was riding the

big gray Bill gave him. They say the horse danced when they shot the chief.

(*hugging Annie*)
Honey, don't cry. All the people are watching. Be brave.

Who's gonna tell Bill?

Nobody. There's no point in bothering Bill with that.

Cody removes his knife and holds it high in the air.

Behold "Chief Sitting Bull," who has murdered more white men than any other redskin . . . who has spoiled more white women than any other redskin . . . who accepts Pahaska's challenge because *it is his destiny!*

Halsey holds a long knife above his head and the battle begins. Cody and Halsey dismount and stalk each other on foot. Halsey's long headdress drags behind him.

Cody knocks "Bull" to the dirt and they wrestle as the arena shakes with applause. Cody and Halsey lock knife blades.

Burke looks at the arena action. It is clear that Sitting Bull, Halsey nor any other Indian is a match for Buffalo Bill Cody. Cody reaches down with his long shining knife and cuts the ornate headdress from his foe. He climbs atop the small prop rock and pumps his knife and the headdress in the air triumphantly.

The imitation "Sitting Bull" lies face down in the dirt. Dead.

> BURKE
> (*to no one in particular*)
> Sitting Bull's not dead. Not as long as Buffalo Bill's alive to kill him in every show!

Now, if we were to judge Buffalo Bill's reaction to the news of Sitting Bull's death at Standing Rock, it would be pure speculation. For Buffalo Bill Cody, true showman that he is, derives great and organic pleasure from murdering his version of the feared chief in the intimacy of his own arena three times during the week and twice on Saturdays.

As we view Buffalo Bill displaying his mighty legend from a great distance, somehow the man, the fans, the arena and even the legend are dwarfed by the river, the plains and the mountains beyond. Then on the ridge that overlooks the WILD WEST camp, a small wooden cross and a string of beads come into view, and for an instant the remains of Chief Sitting Bull appear larger than anything else in sight.

> OLD SOLDIER'S VOICE fades in . . .
> My horse went lame and I was sent back to guard the supply wagon . . . I was lost . . . I was lost for three days and three nights in that rough country . . . And when I reached the battleground of the Custer Massacre, I

saw a gruesome sight. The bodies of our American soldiers were all stripped and mutilated by the Sioux squaws. But it's all in the past . . . I won't be here to tell the people about it. I won't live forever. Who the hell gives a damn anyway.

ABOUT THE AUTHORS

ALAN RUDOLPH was born in Los Angeles and began writing shortly afterward. His screenplays include "Breakfast of Champions," from the novel by Kurt Vonnegut, Jr.; "Welcome to L.A.," an original which he also directed; "The Yig Epoxy" and "Buffalo Bill and the Indians or Sitting Bull's History Lesson," both written collaborations with Robert Altman. He is currently living in a Los Angeles canyon with his wife, Joyce.

ROBERT ALTMAN was born in Kansas City, Missouri, and directed many industrial films there. In other cities he has directed "That Cold Day in the Park," "M*A*S*H," "Brewster McCloud," "McCabe and Mrs. Miller," "Images," "The Long Goodbye," "California Split," "Nashville," "Buffalo Bill and the Indians or Sitting Bull's History Lesson" and "The Yig Epoxy." With his wife Kathryn and his sons, Matthew and Bobby, he lives on the Pacific Ocean near Malibu, California.

Bantam Book Catalog

It lists over a thousand money-saving best-sellers originally priced from $3.75 to $15.00 —bestsellers that are yours now for as little as 60¢ to $2.95!

The catalog gives you a great opportunity to build your own private library at huge savings!

So don't delay any longer—send us your name and address and 25¢ (to help defray postage and handling costs).